Secrets of The Fourth Way

Secrets of The Fourth Way

Alan Francis

Beech Hill Publishing Company
Mount Desert, Maine

BEECH HILL PUBLISHING COMPANY
Mount Desert, Maine 04660

© 2016 by Alan Francis

All rights reserved. No part of this book may be reproduced in any form, or by any means, electronic or mechanical, including photo-copy-ing, recording, or by any information storage and retrieval system, without permission in writing from the publisher.

ISBN: 978-0-9908200-7-9

Printed on acid-free paper in the United States of America

Editor: Susan Dent
Cover design by Pamela Trush / Delaney-Designs
Back cover photo of the author by Olga Zakharova

www.beechhillpublishingcompany.com

One day G. Gurdjieff had said that the role of the Fourth Way, this teaching which is neither the way of the monk, nor the yogi, nor the fakir, *is to appear and disappear, after having deposited what was necessary at this moment, in a certain epoch, in a certain place on the Earth.* That this way could blend into society, change form, become an organization, a religion, or disappear.

Another time G. had said that what had been created would disappear by the fourth generation.

—Solange Claustres
BECOMING CONSCIOUS WITH G.I. GURDJIEF

I Corinthians, 13

If I speak in the tongues of mortals and of angels, but do not have love, I am a noisy gong or a clanging cymbal. And if I have prophetic powers, and understand all mysteries and all knowledge, and if I have all faith, so as to remove mountains, but do not have love, I am nothing. If I give away all my possessions, and if I hand over my body so that I may boast, but do not have love, I gain nothing.

Love is patient; love is kind; love is not envious or boastful or arrogant or rude. It does not insist on its own way; it is not irritable or resentful; it does not rejoice in wrongdoing, but rejoices in the truth. It bears all things, believes all things, hopes all things, endures all things.

Love never ends. But as for prophecies, they will come to an end; as for tongues, they will cease; as for knowledge, it will come to an end.

For we know only in part, and we prophesy only in part; but when the complete comes, the partial will come to an end.

When I was a child, I spoke like a child, I thought like a child, I reasoned like a child; when I became an adult, I put an end to childish ways.

For now we see through a glass darkly, but then we will see face to face. Now I know only in part; then I will know fully, even as I have been fully known.

And now faith, hope, and love abide, these three; and the greatest of these is love.

(A paraphrase from New Revised Standard Version Bible: Anglicised Edition, copyright © 1989, 1995)

Acknowledgements

Thank you—

To my family:

Mom and Dad—may they rest in peace.
My brother.

And to all my unknown ancestors.

My sons, Gabriel and Joshua: May they find their own Way to the Light.
Their mother, Shelley.
All who allowed me to learn something of what loves means.

To my Group leaders and near Group leaders in the Work:

The Gurdjieff Foundation 1969–2006—wherein I began this journey.
Jim Flynn, Norma Flynn, Virginia Pursell; also to Keith Whitmore,
Dr. Lester, Dr. Langmuir, Dr. Jack Haer, Dr. Tilo Ulbrecht IAGF.
Many others I will not name here. R.I.P.

To Lord Pentland, Lady Pentland, Paul Reynard, Michel de Salzmann and many others. I will try to Work as you indicated. R.I.P. To Jerry Needleman for urging me to write this book.

To my friends in the Work who have helped me in many ways:

D.C., L.N., J.H., J.N., A.G., S.L., C.M., S.R., K., F.R.,
E.W., J.O., J.I., L.S., J.N.

To all my friends in Russia and Ukraine, in particular those who have helped organize our Work together and those dedicated to Work:

Kate, Lena, Sergey; Gurdjieff Club: Arkady and Tanya Rovner et al.
Olga Zakharova, my wife.
My friends of City of Masters, Kiev

To my Masters in Asian Arts:

Master Marshall Ho'o, Master Ju Kim Shek, and Master Kai Ying Tung – my everlasting gratitude.
Don Miguel and Dona Anne and White Bear Fredericks.

To my Editor:
Susan Dent
And Publisher:
Ben Elias and Penelope Elias, without whom this book would still be a dusty manuscript among many.

Finally to my teacher George Ivanovitch Gurdjieff who died one month before I was born, to whom I dedicate this book and the return of his work, ten years post, to Russia where it began over a hundred years ago.

—Alan Francis

Contents

Preface

Part I

What were this avatar's last thoughts before he died, having drunk life to the fullest, having experienced the profoundest of visions: deep remorse, lust, sorrow, happiness, wisdom, folly, anxiety over the demands of time and circumstance, perhaps equal measures of hope and despair regarding all human endeavors, the bending and straightening of a man's intent, and finally, the realization that there is time no longer? In those final moments when everything he struggled to attain for himself and humanity rose up to meet him, did the powers and principalities hold their breath as the master juggler began his final act?

As with that agonizing, transcendent shock when Arjuna, surveying massive opposing armies arrayed on the field of battle, turned to Krishna, did Gurdjieff also turn to his own innermost voice and hear the words—words that cannot be spoken, that lose their meaning as soon as they proceed from the mouth of man?

Have you felt this a little? Forsaken, the *I* thirsts in the wilderness; water unexpectedly bursts forth out of desert rock. Who are you, o Seeker? Have you found what you are seeking? Seeking too much, did you listen too little? Behind the thousand faces, on this field of dreams, there is an unchanging one.

We have sought to separate the course from the fine, and in the attempt, we discover we are truly both. We start again; this time from a simple openness, a readiness to touch the ground of our Being. We are just ordinary men and women; it is okay, nothing special here. Yet we find there is a rare dignity, a genuine authority when we truly accept this human state of being. Some of our fear begins to subside; it is a relief—I am just an ordinary man. I lose my way, and I can find it again; it is right here; it cannot go far because it abides in this simple presence that I practice.

It is like misplacing your shoes; then ah, there they are—right where I left them! No one stole them, and no one can take your place. It is right here, where you are now, reading these words. Closer than anything you can put on, closer than your thought, it is *I am*. It is the normal state of *being*, the state of becoming a Man.

We find ourselves drawn to the same sentiment as Rumi, addressing us as *lovers of leaving*. He tells us:

This is not a caravan
of despair,
Though you have broken your vow a thousand times,
Come, come again.

. . . and in finding that courage to continue, we may become emissaries of the unspoken word.

Part II

In common, we share a pauper's existence; an existence consisting almost solely of reflections within a self-inscribed bubble of expectations; this bubble bends the force of consciousness away from our essence. The shocks of life do not on their own create the conditions needed for change. Can we be sufficiently prepared, so that the force of the shock will serve to elicit a fully conscious stop, a denouement in this perpetual play of smoke and shadow, requiring of us serious, might I say, soul searching?

What is the meaning of my life? My life . . . yes, I never really think like that. Now we are speaking about our Work in this life. One might say the life within our life, a Work that is dependent on us. Then, this is perhaps much too simple, and I hope you will bear with me, but could we say that the life of the Work is our Work? Our efforts, our willingness to suffer consciously, feed the body of the Work. If we do not feed the Work, if our understanding does not grow, the understanding of the Work will cease to grow, perhaps cease to exist.

The Work must hold sacred what has been given, but what does that mean? Gurdjieff said, "*If take, take.*" When we have taken our fill what will we give? Will we be like the Pharisees who, having been given the keys, refused to use them and refused to give them to others? When do we begin to see that it is we who owe; it is we who must pay?

We are not talking about a *Pollyannaish* type of altruism. So how do we understand the reciprocal nature of *Being Partkdolg-duty*? Perhaps, at our level we can start by genuinely participating in the three lines of Work: one line on Work on oneself, one line on Work with others, and one line on Work for the Work itself. Then, we may begin to see, to actually experience, that this debt is not a burden; it is a help.

The nature of this help is in the demand to Work, to pay for one's arising and further evolution, so that no conscious effort is in vain. It means we have begun to understand, to perceive the missing link to the level above. This perception is connected to faith in consciousness, or, to put it bluntly, faith. The term "blind faith," that much misunderstood oxymoron, exists for a reason. It is faith without consciousness. Our ordinary self may be third force blind, but there is more to us than that.

Calling the Question

Can the esoteric coherence of Mr. Gurdjieff's stream survive its introduction and dispersal in the open marketplace? How to practice Christ's admonitions, "Do not cast pearls before swine" as well as, "Do not hide your light under a bushel"?

The question of making the Work more available, of becoming Fishers of Men, forces me to consider the likely degradation of our work, that is, the stagnation and degradation that will result from not giving, not feeding those who hunger for what Mr. Gurdjieff has given us, from not circulating the Good. *If give, then give.*

Gurdjieff said, *"I wished to create around myself conditions in which man would be continually reminded of the sense and aim of his existence by an unavoidable friction between his conscience and the automatic manifestations of his nature."*

As Maurice Nicoll said, sin means missing the Mark. And no one is going to say we have hit the Mark; at least I won't say it. So the question is, where have we erred, and how can we return to a more intelligent, sincere search?

When Jesus showed his disciples that they had left the Way in order to dispute who would be first among them, one can only imagine the remorse, the shock that ensued. Having stunned the disciples and their own *legion of I's* into silence, Jesus immediately called for the little children, that is, *essence* to draw nearer.

He tells the disciples that the first shall be last, that he who would be first will be the one who serves; in other words, sacrifice your self-love. Continuing in Work terms, he used this intentional shock to make them Work on themselves. The mind must repent, be aroused to a new thought, causing the maturing *I* to relate more honestly and directly to essence and essence to be guided by one's own inner voice, conscience.

Gurdjieff gives us very clear and poignant examples of his own states of remorse, followed by a change of mind, attitudes, and actions. If we are followers, wishing to emulate, not imitate, then we must honestly assess how we ourselves have been trying to work. What is real Work? After honest reflection, we need to take whatever steps are necessary to return to the Way.

Part III

For many years now, I have sought out and spoken to people who actually knew Gurdjieff, and others whom I respect for their dedication to the Work. Of course I asked them questions that were important to me personally, but I also tried to find out what in the Work was most vital for them. What was, in their opinion, the most important idea, method, form, direction, meaning, and how did they weight them? Finally, what was the sense and aim of this Work? Why does it, and why should it, continue to exist? What is, as Michel de Salzmann asked, *the specificity of the Work?* What does the Work touch and develop that the many other teachings do not?

This inquiry inevitably led to trying to understand this particular phase of our Work and what is required of you and me if the Work is to evolve, that is, to continue. This moment is connected with the whole life of the Work, yet it cannot all be lumped together. It is like building a house or raising a child; each phase must be attended to and respected.

In trying to understand this, we inevitably touch upon the *Deus ex Machina* of our Work; that is, the Enneagram, the pondering machine. It is something I have experimented with for many years; not to make the Enneagram into a crystal ball or personality game but simply to try to help my thinking rise a little in this octave of thought.

Any attempt to explain the Enneagram would be like speaking of the importance of strenuous conscious physical labor, then taking the shovel out of someone's hands. The whole point is to learn how to think. *Learn how to think.* More specifically, to enter life's inner design, to feel it moving, a living and transforming everything. To study myself from each angle and phase, seeing as much of the whole as I can from that viewpoint; then taking another and another, until thought becomes denser and takes on more life. From this fresh look at myself, I begin to feel that my life is not altogether hopeless; each view provides, if I wish to go further, a port of entry into a very Work-able and interesting situation, this situation I call my life.

However, the majority of Mr. Gurdjieff's ideas remain in the books, and the books on the shelves. We extract one that is appealing, "Ah, I like this idea of self-remembering but external considering is really unappealing, and especially with the people I have to work with. . ." Then we find that external considering may be the precise help we need to remember ourselves.

Connected in theory, we begin to be able to conceptualize our Work. This is good, just what we need, both a help and a trap. If we are going to find the way forward, we must make the effort to establish a relationship with these ideas through our Work in everyday life.

You see, it is just here, in and amidst my negativity, my imaginings, my drawers of labels and dreams and all my identifications that I begin to awaken. I don't want to leave here. I don't want to go off and discover a Way. I want to be here. This is where the Enneagram comes in, not an engaging diagram, but rather this alchemical process that can begin now in my life. The process must be undertaken as this whole show goes on and on. But we must find a place to begin, a Do.

Speaking of beginning, it is strange to say that many years ago a plate of cookies and dates changed my life. I was ushered into a room; seven or eight other young people stood side by side in a line. Then a being walked, rather he en-tranced the room; he moved and looked like Nijinsky as Pan or like a being not of this Earth. Quite suddenly and unexpectedly, like Alice, I fell down a rabbit hole, and this then was my introduction to Lord John Pentland.

He started at the front of the line with a small dish of dates and cookies, offering to each person, and each person politely took something: a date for one, a cookie for another.

What, . . ., were they all mad? I thought, as I watched them munch quietly. *Are they completely mad, acting as if we were still in the same dull world as a moment before? Didn't they see what was going on? Couldn't they feel that the air was suddenly dense with vibration?*

When he came to me, I was like a cat at a mouse hole. I had the best seat in town, and it seemed at that moment anything could happen. What wonder might emerge? I was not about to go for the cookie or the date, no sleight of hand for me. Nothing, you see, was going to shake my concentration. He went on . . . a cookie, a date? Then, he returned to where I was standing and asked why I had not taken one. I said, "*I am not hungry.*" We both knew that was not it.

He said to me, "You need to be able to give and take at the same time."

That is how a teacher taught and how a plate of cookies and dates can change your life.

Consider these things:

Whether you give or take, when it evokes suffering in you, perhaps prompted by external considering, when giving is difficult, or you take when it goes against self-love, pride, or vanity, then you are burning away what covers essence, entering the fire of intentional suffering.

Do not make foolish demands for things you have not earned by the sweat of your brow. Make an effort; then personal guidance is invoked.

When you have an aim to get from point A to point B and you are in a hurry to get there, that becomes your aim. Then everything seems to get in your way; you don't see this as lawful resistance; and this makes you irritable, absent, angry, lazy. You say, "What's the use?" or "Poor, poor me." All these reactions are sleep inducing subterfuges. Now I begin to see, a little bit, the chief thing that acts as my substitute, a stand-in that always occupies the place of *I am*.

"The quality of what is transmitted depends on the quality of him who transmits it," and, of course, him who receives it. Gurdjieff tells us this; so caveat emptor.

As to what is most important, that is, the state of the Gurdjieff Work, and to, so-to-say "stir-up" in each reader the cognition that it is their personal duty to assure its continuation, along with some digressions into related areas that might interest him or her, that is the subject of this book. It reflects my viewpoint, nothing more and nothing less.

Part IV

You may discover in these pages many powerful points that can light your path ahead and onto the Way. But, despite the sincere protestations of friends and my editor, you will notice a distinct indifference to you my readers in not simply connecting all the dots for you. This lack of filling in the gaps is entirely my fault and will require of you, the reader, something. It's the postage due.

Enneagram of Work History

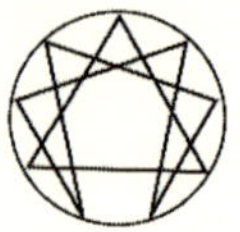

(Gurdjieff's Mission)

0 Do	Gurdjieff's Early Life • Gurdjieff goes to Sarmoung Brotherhood • 1893–1911 Intense preparation for Mission on Earth
1 Re	• G.I. Gurdjieff's Mission: Begin in Russia 1912 • 1911–1932 Gurdjieff begins 21 years artificial life. • 1921 Berlin • First European Lecture
2 Mi	• Gurdjieff forced to leave after lawsuit. • London 1922 • Clash with Ouspensky • England refuses Gurdjieff's visa. • Rejection from Germany and England
3*Shock	Institute for the Harmonious Development of Man
4 Fa	Beginning of new intensive work at the Prieure, in France; primarily Russian, English and American students
5 Sol	• Gurdjieff's nearly fatal auto accident. • Gurdjieff disbands and closes Prieure. • He blames Dark Forces. • Philadelphia, Boston, Chicago–Orage is in charge of "old" American Groups, East Coast, N.Y.

6*Shock Arnel Aoot

- Gurdjieff disputes with Orage and Ouspensky and alienates many of his pupils through his outrageous behavior.
- In HERALD OF THE COMING GOOD he makes strange claims concerning new institute.
- 1927 Gurdjieff contemplates suicide.
- 1929 Stock market crashes.
- 1934 Lama Aghwan Dordjieff dies. Senator Bronson dies.
- Gurdjieff discontinues writing THIRD SERIES and does not continue on the higher bodies of man.
- Gurdjieff requests a return to Russia.
- Stalin's purges begin.
- 1933 Hitler is made chancellor of Germany.
- Orage and Alexander de Salzmann die.
- Gurdjieff dies October 29, 1949, after close work with Initiates and students and after having designated Madame de Salzmann as heir apparent.
- Gurdjieff passes the baton to Initiates.

7 La 1950 Beginning of phase with Gurdjieff's Initiates: The Tracols, Lord Pentland, Madame de Salzmann, and later Michel de Salzmann. New center opens in Caracas, Venezuela spreading throughout South America. Other centers open in Australia and Europe.

8 Si

- 1960's – 90's Eastern teachings appear, especially in California. Lord Pentland begins work in Los Angeles and San Francisco.
- Many pseudo teachers appear.

X 2005 Mr. Gurdjieff's Work returns to Russia.

9 Do The next spiral begins: in 2014. To quote Churchill during World War II: "It is not the end, not even the beginning of the end, but it is the end of the beginning."

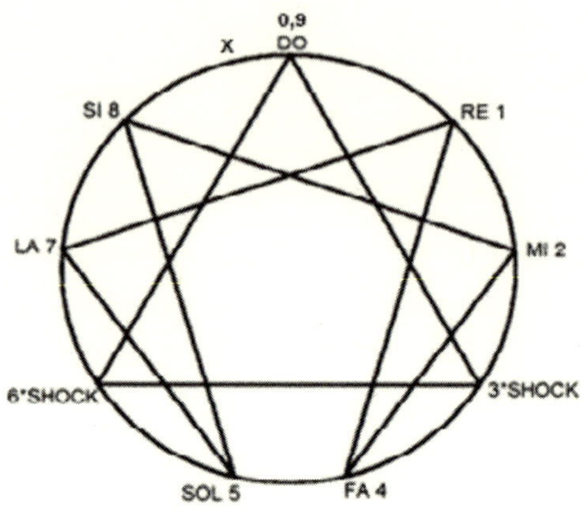

Autobiography

"It propelled me to become what I am."

—Alan Francis

I was born in New York City on November 26, 1949 and raised in Los Angeles, California. My parents were actors.

During my childhood, circumstances in all aspects of daily life were often uncertain, and sometimes they were hazardous, chiefly due to my father's alcoholism. My mother rarely left me alone with my father due to his drinking, but once, when I was a 5 or 6 month old baby, she did leave me with him and took my older brother to a movie. At the theatre, she had a premonition and rushed home with my brother. She was at a movie with my brother, and she rarely got to go places—so for her to get up and come home in time was a miracle. There she found me lying on my back with head wedged between two beds. I was not breathing, and I had turned blue. My father had passed out nearby. My mother, having learned first aid earlier in her life through the Air Force when she worked on wiring bombers, was able to resuscitate me.

But, for me, there were long term effects due to prolonged deprivation of oxygen to my brain. For example, until I reached about the age of 10, I had little to no sensation of physical pain. Also, I had very poor balance, lack of co-ordination, lack of connection to the outer world, and other anomalies. I was definitely cut off from the world and had to make connections.

I could look at other people my age and see that there were things not right with me. I remained alone with these realizations, and it caused a lot of confusion and depression at times. Perhaps through the influence of the way my mother handled the hardships she faced, the deficiencies in myself chiefly stimulated an interest in me in overcoming the retardations and also stimulated a pervasive awareness in me of being a stranger in a strange land. But I did not learn of the traumatic facts of my infancy and of how they came about until I was a teenager—about the time also that my parents divorced and subsequently my father died the sad death of a skid row alcoholic.

Early on I became interested in the meaning of life and in such questions as why am I here? Also, I recall instances of self-remembering. When I was very young, maybe 4 or 5 years old, I had dreams I was sitting in the lotus position in front of a cave in the mountains. And in the dream I was transmuting elements between my palms, mostly fire and water. I had been exposed to nothing esoteric in my family. Since they were actors, my parents did recite as they moved about the house. With my father it was Hamlet's soliloquy. I can still recite that; it was very confusing to me at a young age, "to be or not to be," a man in a very confused state. With my mother, she recited "The Village Blacksmith," and I remember "thus in the burning forge of life, each lesson must be wrought."

I met many different people—actors, gypsies, con artists, Indians, bums and alcoholics. I quickly developed an instinct for self-preservation. In my teens I began karate but soon switched to Tai Chi Chuan, studying with Master Marshall Ho'o and later Master Tung Kai Ying.

This was also a time which I spent immersed in the so-called hippie culture of the 60's. At 19, I also began to study Taoist healing with Master Ju Kim Shek, along with meditation and a continued interest in philosophy and shamanism. I traveled to Mexico to meet with brujos and curanderos. (See chapter entitled "Facts.")

At the same age after several years of searching, I found my first Gurdjieff group leader, Jim Flynn, one of the founders of the Gurdjieff Foundation of Los Angeles under Lord John Pentland. I met Lord Pentland when I was 20; in him I found the first indisputable evidence of a man who lived and understood life at a higher level of being. Later, I met others, including Paul Reynard and especially Dr. Michel de Salzmann whose degree of harmonious development was living and palpable proof to me of the value of Gurdjieff's teachings. Paul Reynard gave me permission to begin Foundation groups; Michel de Salzmann, the leader of the Work worldwide, approved this and added that I would attract more people to the Work and start new centers and gave me specific instructions concerning this.[1]

Returning to my history in 1970's, with a small group of college friends, I began to explore different areas of mutual interest; one friend was interested in Isha Schwaller de Lubicz; another J. Krishnamurti, Chogyam Trungpa—the Phi ratio; several were friends of Carlos Castenada, and so on. The more I explored with my friends, the more I became convinced that Gurdjieff's teachings were the most salient. It re-enforced the strange conviction I had felt when I first began reading IN SEARCH OF THE MIRACULOUS at the age of 16, the certainty that Gurdjieff was the teacher of this age and the one whom I would follow the rest of my life.

My friends and I incorporated the Institute for Taoist Studies in 1971 and seven years later began the first college of Taoist healing. During this period of time in China the Mao Purges were still going on, and all the Masters in Healing, Energy Work, and Meditation were being killed. A few escaped, some to California, and we began efforts to find them and to collect data from 100 Masters of ancient Tao wisdom, whom we found from all over the world including Europe, Vietnam, and Taiwan. I was the chair outreach person for the national training exams which we set up working with the material from these Masters.

In 1986, I became the founding director of Turnaround, a skid row social services center that specialized in the treatment and rehabilitation of alcoholics and drug addicts, many coming directly off the streets or from jail. We began a pilot project to coordinate treatment for a better transition within the county jail to Turnaround. Following this, I co-owned and worked in a remodeling company, was a consultant to business, particularly nonprofits in strategic planning, grant and technical writing, stress and performance improvement, hands-off and mentoring.

I have led seminars and taught Taoist and other related arts since 1972. However, in my Work, teachings and practices are not mixed, and the central focus of my life has always been and still remains the Gurdjieff teachings.

In 2005, I moved outside a small town in the high Sonoran Desert of Arizona and designed and built a small house where I continue to live when I am in the United States. In that same year I began to travel to Russia on a regular schedule and founded an experimental Gurdjieff Group in Moscow, now called the Russian Center for Gurdjieff Studies. In Russia, it is the only Gurdjieff Fourth Way organization in direct lineage from Gurdjieff himself. It is now 10 years since Mr. Gurdjieff's teachings were renewed in Russia.

◊◊◊

I take this present moment in the whole of my Work to prepare for the future shock and repair our past.

Having just now passed through the final stage of a task given to me nearly 14 years ago, and having by law encountered from Si the downward and backward thrust to the Harnel-aoot—where the division between outer and inner forces is particularly acute, I am now obliged to say how it all began.

And why I took on the "impossible task" of returning George Ivanovitch Gurdjieff's Work to the place of its birth. It was a task given to me Michel de Salzmann. When I went to the Foundation, that is, the highest officials, to ask for help in establishing the group in Russia, most were opposed to help in any way.

But now it is done.

How did it all come about? I will begin to describe the historic movement from exo-meso-esoteric school.

Jim Flynn was my leader of the Los Angles Gurdjieff group; when I first became involved, he and his wife Norma led the group together. They worked closely and directly under Lord Pentland, and I met Lord Pentland through them.

After many years of strong animus leadership by Jim Flynn, he abruptly left the Foundation. Lord Pentland was very disappointed as we all were. Jim once told a curious friend of mine, "I come to bear the negative manifestations of others." In my opinion, Jim was the only man in the L.A. Foundation. I guess he had had enough. He and Norma divorced. Norma Flynn, as director of the

L.A. Foundation, gave me the task of starting a group in Oregon, and she became my advisor when I started the Oregon group; it was comprised of 12 or 13 people.

At a point in the existence of this L.A. Foundation group, a secret group, not sanctioned by the LA Foundation, was formed with the purpose to explore higher being states. I led this group which was comprised of selected members of our L.A. group and some leaders in the L.A. Foundation. We met in a private home. The meetings were held outside the domain of the Los Angeles Foundation. It was advised directly by Norma Flynn who in turn was advised regarding this group by Michel de Salzmann and Paul Reynard. It was the beginning of separate work from the Foundation condoned by my teachers.

Now, Jim and Norma Flynn are both deceased. But I am looking backwards as I write in the autumn of 2014 to tell this history.

NOTES

[1] From the notes of Alan Francis, Los Angeles, California, 1999.

My Work with Alan Francis

by Elena Tushina

The following essay was written by Russian psychologist, Elena Tushina, who is one of Alan Francis' students in his Moscow Gurdjieff Group. She wrote it originally in Russian and later translated it herself into English. The only editing done to the manuscript is in places where the meaning in English needed to be clarified.

I first met Alan in February 2007. One of my friends, knowing that I was interested in Mr. Gurdjieff's teaching, told me about the lecture given by Alan Francis. Before that I had read some books by Ouspensky and his followers (for example, Rodney Collin), "Meetings with Remarkable Men" by Gurdjieff etc., and therefore I was in a sense familiar with the ideas and terminology of the system, of course superficially. I was very attracted by Gurdjieff's ideas, his cosmology, introduced by Ouspensky; I felt that here it was possible to find answers on such questions as the aim and purpose of the human life, the meaning of everything existing, the methods to study oneself and the world, transformation—questions of interest probably for everyone searching for this way. At the same time even from the books it was possible to feel the power and boundlessness of Gurdjieff's Teaching as well as the great difference between him and other people, in the sense of being. On the other side, I had also felt that nothing would come free, that it could cost me something that was difficult to abandon. So this friction between the wish to know and understand, a search for the answers, and a vague anxiety from the presentiment of something new, created an impulse to the further search, which resulted in the encounter with Alan and the group working under his guidance.

I remember this first impression very well—I had entered the room full of strange people about 10 minutes before the start. Some people were standing in small groups talking, moving here and there; some were sitting already at their places—as always in a well-attended meeting. Alan was sitting on the chair in the depth of the room where the stage is usually placed. And this difference was very visible—between moving and talking people and one man sitting in silence. He was sitting very straight but not tense and was very quiet, really quiet, and stillness was surrounding him. In my life I have met many people who had attained something in their lives, quite extraordinary people, charismatic, strong, and with outstanding qualities; and I do remember them and have respect toward them up to now, but I have never seen such inner silence and concentration as Alan had shown.

After the lecture I asked the administrator if there would be more events with Alan. It appeared that there was an open Gurdjieff seminar planned for the following weekend. Then one day Alan had a personal talk with me, and soon I was included into his group.

When I entered the group I was like that woman from the story of Anna Butkovskaya, who came to Gurdjieff in Paris with the heap of dresses and furs, and the Master at once had shown to her the uselessness of all those. To some extent it was not so difficult to me to part with this image of myself, but the vanity is a quality to work upon during all my life. It is so treacherous and able to hide beyond the other minor "i"s which sometimes are hard to notice.

I have one strong memory: once I took Alan to his home after a group meeting (I was quite a reckless driver that time). A guy in an old white Russian car had cut into my lane so I had to press the brakes fast. Then when I had passed his car, I drove back, pulling over in front of him, and then rushed away. Such a manoeuvre! Alan slapped me on the shoulder and said: "Well now I know one more side of you." And that was like a shock for me. Now those words are like a reminding factor—often when I see inside this foolish excitement of the emotions mixed with my features, I remember those words.

In the beginning the weekly meetings had caused a resistance in me. I could not understand the necessity to meet so often and moreover the necessity of the retreats every 2-3 months. Then I just start attending the meetings. Sometimes I came to a meeting and sat without a word not understanding what to say and why.

And I can tell now that this understanding did not come in one moment; it grew little by little. The Retreats as an intensive practice are very useful—the energy becomes concentrated, vibrations become higher, and the understanding of the ideas and phenomena grow. At the same time continuous, consistent efforts of regular meetings are also necessary. Once Alan said about it—that the consistency of weekly meetings is not less (and may be even more) important than participation in a two-day seminar. It is always so useful to see my resistance toward the group meetings (that could be both inner and outer resistance—for example, seeking for the reasons for not getting there, or the resistance during the meeting itself)—this is always an impression of myself, the field to work upon, the chance to step back from my ego.

There were more than 20 people in the group when I joined it. Then some people left, new ones came and went away, some stayed. And, of course, we are connected by a special connection that is neither friendship nor family ties. It is different, and it gives warmth to me. Working in this group is not something static; it is a constant search towards something to have my mind and feelings open. This is a continuous practice to awaken from my own sleep—moment after moment. Every group meeting is a concentrated life experience. Where else could I see my illusions so completely? Or meet with my negative parts and become aware of them? Has someone in his ordinary life an idea how to see his own ugliness and powerlessness? On the contrary, as psychologists say, our psychology tries to protect us from this unattractive picture of ourselves as best as it can. Self-excuse is very common for a contemporary man. Sometimes I see this self-excusing "i" trying to come to the surface in the case of some failure.

Why does one want to know oneself? We cannot make it our task to get rid of a certain feature because the placing of this question itself already presumes that we know, but we do not know. First we should study. We can only observe. And the process of observation and the attempts to understand what this observation is—this process is an endless search and intrigue.

I remember my first retreat very well. It took place in one of the beautiful places not far from Moscow; the group was almost in a full complement. That was not my first experience of group work (I took part in many psychological trainings before I met

Alan, and some methods were similar, but the emphasis and aims were different, and the presence and guidance of Alan, of course, were not there). There was a lot of physical labor; we were cooking and washing everything; also there was a practice of Gurdjieff Movements. In the end of the day, when I was out of forces, there also was sitting. And also Alan was working individually with everyone. I asked Alan how he saw me and my work in the group; he said that he did not know me well enough yet because I was new, but he saw that I was very closed and I had to learn to be open. It was not quite clear for me, and I did not agree; I did not consider myself so closed, and I left this question hanging somewhere inside, but I remembered about that. Within several years I understood that this closedness is impossible to just remove. It will go away when the power of ego weakens. How do I understand that it has weakened?—when I stop comparing and judging, when I stop thinking that I'm right. (Once at an open meeting Alan said that this conviction that "I'm right" is a criterion of the false part of oneself, and he has repeated that especially for me, because it was difficult for me to agree).

Once we went out for the retreat to one of the most interesting places in the Caucasus Mountains, in the south of Russia. There also was a lot of practice—physical labor, exercises, sittings, special tasks. On one of the days of the retreat, we were gathering flat stones at the riverbed and making a path, trying to work on an exercise at the same time; and Alan was also answering our questions. Everyone who felt the necessity could ask a question. This picture—how we were sitting over there all together—is still in front of my eyes. And Alan said to me again: "You have to let go of your fear to be open." This is a question for me to investigate what it means to me—to be open.

Within all those years I have never heard a word of Alan blaming someone; neither have I heard from him sharp judgments—although he can be very strict when it's necessary. At that retreat mentioned above on one wonderful cool morning we were sitting in the forest trying to follow Alan's words. And suddenly a dog ran up to us; it was looking very happy and joyful, and it tried to make us play with it. And our attention had switched over to the dog immediately. Everyone it came up to had shown a reaction. All of a sudden Alan shouted: "That's it. We are gone. What is the value of your attention if everything distracts it?" And we did not return to the sitting that morning. This is true—there are thousands of distractions of every kind; everything tries to eat our attention. But the attention—it is what we need so much. We cannot do, but we can become able to direct our attention.

One of the brightest experiences, in my opinion, was the staging of the Myth of Isis and Osiris. Alan told this legend briefly to us and assigned the roles. Mine was Isis. How had he guessed that it was so important to me? I had to live through and realize that a woman with endless patience gathers, creates, and brings life. In total, it's difficult for me to compare the power of impressions of the participation in this mystery to anything else. We had rehearsed our words, gestures and postures, but when the performance started, everything changed; it seemed we understood each other without words; there was a complete silence in the room. I could say that the feeling of the support and understanding was sensed not only within us but also from the spectators. To experience and feel this wise creative part of myself, as well as the power and support of the other parts, or power and deceit of someone else's part, to realize all this complexity and the necessity of the efforts and sacrifice before something new could appear, having another being, power and resources—that was the main experience for me in this internal drama, so nicely performed.

All the Work for me consists of such gleamings of understanding. Four years passed before I saw my disunity, multiplicity of my "I's" and realized how difficult it is to give up some of them (for example, the "i" that thinks that it has a right to judge the others, or the "i" that thinks it knows something better). In the six and a half years after starting work in Alan's group, I saw that "I" is not my functions, or, to put it more precisely, I had an experience of the division of the "I" and the other, functional parts of myself. I should say that this understanding appeared in the result of one of the group exercises given to us by Alan. And this experience became even stronger after the seminar in the summer (2013). For me it was a real intensive work period with the result that I had the chance to experience something both new and familiar. I do not know if that was my own "I," (maybe just a taste of it), and it was full of life. Together with useful discoveries, individual experience, expanded attention, efforts to be present, feeling of the real life, it also was possible to see how the Masters work. Here perhaps the meaning of the idea of doing could be seen, couldn't it?

Who is Alan for me? A man, crystallized in the Work, with endless patience and love. Once after one difficult group meeting I asked Alan in the e-mail exchange, something like: "how are you able to bear all this silliness, ignorance and laziness existing in us all the time?" And he answered very simply: "Because I know deep inside there is a light within you, and slowly it begins to burn more brightly."

Is the Teaching of Gurdjieff mostly a psychological system? I say both yes and no, because it is wider than any existing system. And probably it is impossible to understand it from the level of my ordinary mind, from the mind which thinks that it is the master, or does not think at all. And how to develop the other mind, to come in contact with that really intelligent part of myself? For me, the answer here is in a long way of patience and confidence in people whose being is different than my own.

Candor

Why is it I never come to the heart of the matter? I talk incessantly but never speak what is true. What is true? Even the words sound hollow.

What have I become that truth can find no resonance in me? I am not able to accept the clear inference arising from this experience.

I can easily rationalize my way out of this, by admitting that my words are merely labels for things, and that is why voicing them causes no vital reaction within me. Yet, if my words are not true, then whom do they represent? In effect, I am asking, who is speaking?

So far this inquiry seems to be leading me nowhere. I tried to free myself from the burden of seeing that my words are empty, but instead my question pulls me deeper, and I feel more than ever that my words and actions should be yoked to something. I am intrigued, curious to see where this might lead.

I began with the idea of candor, a word sharing its root with incandescence and candle. Some believe that candor comes when we are least attentive, in the off the cuff remark, the word said in angry haste, the Freudian slip, which marks truth-saying as an accident. There may be occasions when a suppressed feeling or opinion is revealed accidentally, but that hardly constitutes a movement towards truth.

Gurdjieff points to how our thinking process has been turned upside down. For example, take the term self-conscious: "I spilled gravy on my tie, and that made me self-conscious." Here is a clear example of how words have lost their meaning, turned into their opposites. Candor also has lost its true meaning.

Candor arises when one intentionally throws light on a situation. It leaves little room for emotional exhibitionism, fake humility, or the phony frankness of the talk show.

Gurdjieff tells us that being sincere in a Group and with one's teachers on the Way is a necessity. A Group, maturing slowly, must nurture trust and discretion. A pretense of sincerity, where one indiscriminately exposes ones underbelly in public like a dog, is a sign of weakness and stupidity.

Gurdjieff also gives special emphasis to Work conditions, which allow new influences to enter. From one viewpoint, the whole of the Work is nothing more and nothing less than a set of, sometimes artificial, at other times, more organic, conditions, continually being drawn from the confluence of cosmic forces and the dual demands of human need.

What then are the conditions that can evoke candor? What can bring me to a deep and genuine moment, when I would feel remorse if I were to respond other than with complete sincerity?

I don't know if Gurdjieff used the word candor, but I think he would have liked it. On the related subject of conscience, Gurdjieff has given a number of indications as to its place, contents, and function.

It has been said that conscience is the only thing within us that is not relative and that the emergence of conscience will illuminate, perhaps very painfully, all the contradictions we have inside. We need to see how practicing candor can act as a preparation for the emergence of genuine being conscience.

If sincerity represents the heart's search for truth, then perhaps candor is the state in which the critical mind becomes the heart's partner in this search. To form a stable triad, such a search would need to be physically grounded in an instinctive sensing of reality.

Is the word candor quietly slipping from our everyday language? Is it possible that the art of candor will be thoroughly replaced by the equally powerful "art" of gossip?

Gossip, one could say, is the representative of false personality. It can only exist when the false image of oneself is dominant, when the feeling of a false and malignant superiority is allowed to control essence. One cannot sit in judgment without these I's occupying that same seat of power. Like candor, gossip also acts as a sword; yet there is no healing in it, no search for what is true.

Candor must always stand in firm opposition to gossip. Gossip spreads like a plague and is hard to eradicate, as it hides behind all kinds of benign masks. In contrast, it is striking to observe the therapeutic effect of talking with even one other person who strives to speak with candor. Yes, it is a rare event.

There seems to be no single word in common usage that communicates the power, vulnerability, and intensity required in a search for truth. Candor, with its fully resurrected meaning of an incandescent state, may fill that void. Thus the idea of candor, applied in Work conditions, may set our inner life aflame, illuminating our search.

Enneagram: The Fundamental Steps to Mastery

Outer Circulation

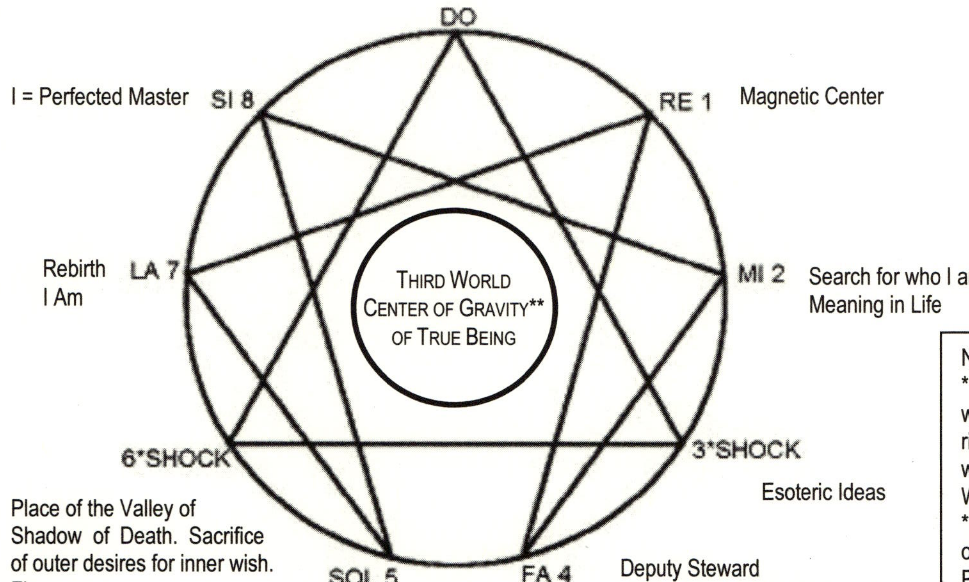

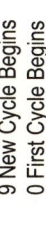

Inner Circulation

1 to 4 Crystallization

4 to 2 Focuses

2 to 8 Culmination

8 to 5 Creates in anticipation

5 to 7 Chrysalis

7 to 1 Return for further purification

NOTES

* From outside is first part of enneagram, i.e., left wing (stage left or mirror image); and from inside is right wing. The reference here is to the shape of wings, like the Archangel Michael who protects the Way, or if you prefer, protective like a mother bird.

**Holding all together, inward pull opposes outward centrifugal forces of Time. See Energy Pathways Handbook. We have two things again: one is psychological represented here, the other is energetic. Psychology appears where Sol becomes Do for the lateral octave.

The Seeker and Addiction

G. I. Gurdjieff suggests that we go out on a dark starry night, and, looking up into that vast infinite space ask ourselves, "Is what we want simply madness?"

All of us who search for meaning in our lives will face an insurmountable obstacle, an obstacle we can neither go around nor climb over: the sword of ego, that *bully-boy* we so often employ in these moments. The sword cannot cut this "Gordian Knot," as it protects its own.

Here I will draw for you a brief sketch of that obstacle, as seen from the viewpoint of Gurdjieff's Fourth Way Work and perhaps surprisingly, from the viewpoint of the Twelve Step Program.

G. I. Gurdjieff said we live as prisoners held in trance-like sleep, a state of diminished consciousness, a consequence of a psychic-organic fixation called *Kundabuffer*. Kundabuffer acts like a jamming mechanism preventing normal perception and consequently normal thought and action.

The Twelve-Step concept, initially applied in Alcoholics Anonymous, has expanded to include other disorders as well as alcoholism. It is now generally recognized that a wide range of compulsive "dis-ease" based habit patterns should be treated as addictions.

Inquiry

Are these destructive behavioral patterns "biologically hardwired," and if so, how did that happen? Is that why they are so strangely resilient and resistant to change?

Why should a therapeutic approach to addiction be introduced into the ongoing discussion of human potential? In particular, why should it come up in a discussion of the higher possibilities, which may be found throughout Mr. Gurdjieff's Work?

Comparison

There are some striking parallels and many differences between these two methods. One is clearly more exoteric, the other esoteric. However, fundamentally, they are both practical means to come to the aid of an enslaved humanity.

Twelve Steps focuses on changing life-threatening behavior through realizing one's powerlessness and invoking help of a higher power. Twelve Steps provides a means by which addicts can stop using and begin living a healthier life.

Further along, real progress in Gurdjieff's three-centered, seven-tiered Work depends on a growing understanding of what it means to act as conscious human beings. For some people, it may be indispensable to be an active member of both.

Since leaders in the Gurdjieff Work are seldom trained as healers or counselors, they may not be adept in dealing with health and "addiction" issues or in understanding the relationship of these issues to every seeker.

> THE SEEKER:
> What did I want when I set out in search of the truth? The very beginning was full of hope and a wish to work at any cost. But despite the importance of this wish to begin, I had far too little preparation. I easily lose heart when I come up against real difficulty.

Addiction

The word addiction comes from the Latin *addictus*, meaning assigned by decree, pledged, or made over to. In a sense, I have unknowingly pledged myself, but to what? It is as though a "parasitical" organism is feeding off my life, the inevitable result of the consequences of the organ *Kundabuffer*, which Gurdjieff says, was implanted in the base of the spine of our ancestors to keep them asleep and docile.

Independently supporting the above premise, the Yogi Desikachar, following the teachings of the Great Indian Sage Patanjali, gives a clear description of the coiled serpent Kundalini and how it prevents the intelligent life force, Prana, from initiating normal transformation.

In his book, RELIGIOUSNESS IN YOGA, Desikachar clarifies that Kundalini is a knot or blockage, which deflects normal Pranic flow from the main channel or Susumna. Without this obstruction, the potential natural evolution of human consciousness, still qualified by choice, would be unimpeded by self-generated illusion, a projection of this same Kundalini. This view clearly reinforces Gurdjieff's assertions.

Gurdjieff compares the effect of the influence of Kundalini to cocaine addiction, citing it as the fundamental cause of our hypnotic sleep. Both Desikachar and Gurdjieff indicate the necessity of a carefully graduated burning or dissolving of this obstruction. This alone will allow the initiation of a normal completing relationship with Prana, the life force.

This *knot* interferes first with basic perceptual function; from there, it generates a false self-image, false personality, chief feature, and then, as a false idolatry, it invades our psyche. This process may be further exacerbated by certain misguided energy practices, as well as by drugs, that stimulate Kundalini. These practices induce perverse energy to rise through the central channel, infecting higher centers.

However, even without this catalyst, the difference between a sane man and a madman is often only a matter of circumstance. Every day we see supposedly sane people do insane things. We all unconsciously contribute to the social circumstance, this social disease, by radiating negativity which becomes a poisonous leaven in society. The eminent psychiatrist Wilhelm Reich referred to this unconscious dissemination of aberrant life energy as an "emotional plague."

Inwardly, this "emotional plague" attaches itself to one of many false '*I's*' as vectors for spreading this disease within the person. This potentiates and magnifies "*I-dentification*," and gives it a subtle social rationale, as it has become an accepted substitute for what should be normal behavior. The resulting psychological changes are more easily recognized in the exaggerated behavior of cocaine addicts.

However, at times we are all infected, pathologically stimulated, and then fall into "depressed" states. The resulting vacuum and depletion of a naturally occurring opiate or neurohormone like dopamine can then automatically precipitate another round.

Each of us has his/her own personal form of self or, in Gurdjieffian terms, *essence* abuse. We may of course deny this awkward truth and embrace a rationalization. Why not go back to the comforting thought that an addict simply means someone addicted to drugs? No? What then is addiction? Perhaps we could try out a new definition, which may reveal a disturbing continuum: ***Addiction is the crystallization of identification.***

Identification

> *In the East where people smoke hashish and other drugs it often happens that a man becomes so identified with his pipe that he begins to consider that he is a pipe himself. This is not a joke but a fact. He actually becomes a pipe. This is identifying. And for this, hashish and opium are entirely unnecessary. Look at people in shops, in theatres and restaurants, or see how they identify with words when they argue about something or try to prove something, particularly something they do not know themselves. They become greediness, desires, or words; of themselves nothing remains.*
>
> Gurdjieff quoted in IN SEARCH OF THE MIRACULOUS by P. D. Ouspensky. Later, he adds, "*Identifying is the chief obstacle to self-remembering.*"

What is identification? Enslaved by the power, I give over to *false personality* through identification; I begin to see that it holds sway over every detail of my life. If it were simply a matter of choice, why have I not chosen to awaken?

I am unable to free myself from identification. Is this not the road to addiction? The addict is powerless. Is this not what

Gurdjieff means when he says that man has no will? In order for transformation to take place, some of the sacred Prana found in my head, heart, and spine must be set apart for the purpose of inner growth. The energy contained in the seeker's "wish to be," must not be sidetracked by every transient, externally focused desire.

To avoid this loss of power we need to understand a pivotal inner mechanism, a mechanism allied to a deeply held belief that falsely empowers fractions of myself to act as "I." Take, for example, "I am hot!," "I know better!," or "I am angry!" A tiny "I," having momentarily climbed to the top of the heap, is declaring, "I am King of the Mountain!"

Then, for the briefest glorious moment, it usurps total control, saying, "I am!" until the next moment when "I am hungry!" replaces "I am pissed off at the driver in front of me!" Repetitive "I" mantras, like these, lead to psychological fixation and perceptual opacity. Thus, I surrender my whole life for a trifle.

"Struth! What might not happen in this world. A flea might swallow an elephant."[1]

What would make it possible to participate in a cosmic exchange of energies and yet still retain individuality? First, I must consciously strengthen non-desire, physically cordoning it off from desire.

Twelve Steps and The Fourth Way

Poets, writers, artists, dancers, creative thinkers, and cutting-edge seekers are more likely than other people to suffer from depression or manic states. Some are bi-polar, balancing precariously between extremes, highly susceptible to any nostrum that offers brief oblivion.

Some of Gurdjieff's highest level and most intelligent students, such as P.D. Ouspensky, Alexandre De Salzmann, and Rene Daumal, suffered greatly and may have died prematurely as a result of drugs or alcohol. Gurdjieff spoke frankly of his own "black and madcap" states. Unfortunately, since Gurdjieff's death, the subject of addiction, psychopathology, and the very real perils facing the seeker are seldom, if ever, addressed.

Today, there are seekers in many spiritual disciplines, including the Gurdjieff Work, who may have been saved from self-destruction by Twelve-Step Programs. Although there is little statistical validation for its effectiveness, strong anecdotal evidence exists.

The Twelve Steps, the sponsor relationship, and the group format have been utilized to help resolve cocaine, smoking, gambling, eating, sex and other chemical/behavioral addictions. These programs may be a kind of quasi-religious form of heart-centered work.

Based in faith and submission to a higher power, Twelve Steps seems closer to the Way of the Monk than to Gurdjieff's Fourth Way. However, those on the Fourth Way must also bend the knee and pass under a low threshold. While conscious egoism may serve as a motivation to bring me to a certain crossroads, eventually it too must die.

Wounds

On an ordinary psychological level, a trauma, or undigested shock, often sets in motion dissociative reactions. This fragmentation may become the seed of further pathological patterns, and, in extreme cases, even may result in a multiple personality disorder. The emotionally painful experience is isolated and may immure a new personality fragment. These fragments then aggregate. Amassing through a false idea of myself or strong negative emotion, through imagination, they then become connected with chief feature, occupying the center of gravity of my mechanical existence. Perhaps, herein lies the secret genesis of our ape-like chief feature, drawn from a pacified essence mixed with our false image and protected by an army of little I's.

Gurdjieff asserts that we live not as one unified person, but in a state of many separate "I"s. Does that refer to the result of this same process? Isn't what we call normality simply less severe dissociation, activating the very same mechanism to build walls or "shock absorbers" between the many "I's" in myself? Like divisions in a honeycomb, mini-buffers are erected to feed and protect fragments of myself from further psychological pain and to insure continued dominance of an infantile pleasure principle.

Perhaps the only difference between our normal state now and utter dissociation is a trace of memory, a bit of substance, a contact point between these otherwise isolated "I's" in myself. And is there no alternative to this splintered identity? Gurdjieff provides one powerful answer: self-remembering. Could I then offer the whole of myself to this inner transformation, and if so, how? Can I intentionally absorb my reactions by attending directly to the shock, allowing not a hairsbreadth to stand between my attention and my life?

Why accept a slap in the face, why turn the other cheek, if not for the understanding that it is here that *I* may appear; or, is it here that *I* may lose my way? It is up to me. An outer shock, perhaps a criticism, perhaps a glance from one who knows, may then be met with an attention and awareness capable of bearing a vital substance on its inward journey. Working from within, I watch for the shock sparked from that friction of inquiry between "What do I want?" and "What am I lacking now?" Then the energy from this shock is induced to re-enforce the line of an inner octave of impressions through its next interval.

Towards Balance

Ordinary personality is a marvel, designed to insure a mechanical homeostatic equilibrium filling the gap between organism and environment. Formed of tactical defenses, rationalizations, instinctive mechanisms, it is a circus dedicated to the status quo. This equilibrium is counterpoint to the seeker in me, who desperately searches for meaning. Like the Fool in the Tarot, the addict, having lost all, looks into the abyss and feels the impact of reality crashing through his dream "I."

The seeker who is fortunate enough to find the Work may not have had such a dramatic realization. He may have had neither a sufficient shock to loosen the hold of self-importance, nor the agony and epiphany, the taste of organic shame, in standing before others and saying, "I am Bill W., and I'm an alcoholic."

As outlined in IN SEARCH OF THE MIRACULOUS, the stages of the Work are *waking, dying, and resurrection.* The spiritual awakening and the death of the addict come from that impact of hitting bottom. In the Gurdjieff Work, intentionally created artificial conditions are required to shock the Seeker, so he can bite through to the bone and get to the real world.

And all our yesterdays have lighted fools
The way to dusty death. Out, out brief candle!
Life's but a walking shadow, a poor player
That struts and frets his hour upon the stage
And then is heard no more. It is a tale
Told by an idiot, full of sound and fury,
Signifying nothing.[2]

Or perhaps he can slide by, never really confronting his chief feature. Will he then be in the Work but not of it? Gurdjieff told one man that he always argued. The man heatedly replied, "But then I never argue!" Invisible to us, chief feature, the controlling agent of my slavery, is an image both jealously and blindly guarded.

Spiritual War

In order to start a real inner search, it is first necessary to be tipped off balance. The recovering addict is off balance, and in the Twelve Step Program, by surrendering to a "higher power," the addict chooses life by placing himself on the battlefield of a war he must win. In this situation, the world can look black and white, the white knight against the black. This simple duality may be necessary for the addict, but it is only a transitional stage in our understanding.

In the Work, opening to the external authority of a teacher, the seeker finds that the uncomfortable conditions beget a struggle between the subjective and more colorful desires of the "body" and the objective non-desire of the incipient soul. For the novice, the nature of this spiritual struggle is hard to understand.

One could say that desire attempts to fulfill our wants and needs by projecting them outward: they are Nature's great motivators and necessary levers for handling external life. Awareness is the feeling that I am already here, fulfilled, so I do not need to look beyond my present situation. The conflict between the two forces forms a useful, that is, *Workable* set of tensions, i.e., tensions that can create the right conditions for self-observation.

Heal Thyself

> *To the same end, this program includes a medical section, since, for many people, it is necessary, before undertaking the development of their natural capacities, to correct first of all the already existent functional disorders, without which it is impossible to achieve productive work aimed at the desired harmonious development.*
>
> *Particular attention will be paid to those individuals who show certain pathological symptoms, such as the weakness of will, "willfulness", laziness, unreasonable fears, a sense of continual fatigue, apathy, irregular exchange of substances, obesity or exhaustion, abuse of alcohol, narcotics, etcetera.*
>
> –*Herald of the Coming Good* by G. I. Gurdfjieff

Have you found yourself here? Perhaps you have also unearthed many such beauties. But who is able to truly diagnose and treat these disorders? Gurdjieff encouraged the involvement of specialists, who had knowledge and experience with mixed substances; the power to heal and the wisdom to direct our efforts toward correcting those shortcomings that he clearly stated make it "*. . . impossible to achieve productive work aimed at the desired harmonious development.*"

Now, I may have heard my diagnosis, "a sleeping, mad machine," but do I accept it? The addict must remember what he is every day. A slip is very visible. With the prognosis of a miserable life and an early death, the aim is self-recovery. However, this large aim is utterly dependent on being "clean and sober" this moment, the next, and the next. With this kind of perpetual demand on attention and will, what an advantage it is to be aware of death awaiting a misstep. Is there a corresponding razor's-edge upon which the seeker must walk?

This question may shed light on why Gurdjieff revealed his own addiction to the power of animal magnetism. According to his account in the Third Series, this power over others had made him

"*. . . spoiled and depraved to the core.*" Yet, sacrificing the loss of this personal power, somehow he turned for something he valued more.

Gurdjieff made it clear that general conditions alone can never touch all sides of a man. Only with the help of individually focused Work can the complex, subjective fixations and disabilities that deflect one's aim at every turn be resolved. This may mean binding inner demons, in whatever form they take, into a true talisman of self-remembering.

Requiem

I drove into the city today. As I was walking down the street, a black man in his sixties glanced up from the shopping cart full of his worldly possessions and boomed, "A drowning man will clutch at a straw!"

"Yes," I replied.

Having appraised me in that brief but quintessential exchange, he continued, "You know what I'm talkin' about don't you?"

I stopped. "Yes, I do."

The above "'material for thought" is offered to the critical mind.

A few additional notes:

The place of addiction on the downward spiral of human life can be further studied in BEEZELBUB'S TALES. For the societal effects, see page 212ff., regarding King Konuzion, and for the more internal effects on the possible arising of conscience, see page 379 ff., regarding Ashiata Shiemash.

Gurdjieff seems to be pointing to a broader continuum here, perhaps the "Terror of the Situation"; from Kundabuffer to the division of consciousness (Zoostat), to ego, to division of society (castes), to the unworthy impulses of haughtiness, servility etc., to the squashing of the impulse of organic shame (which could lead us back towards Conscience), to addiction (Opium, Athenianism etc.), and finally to the creation of a Hasnamuss.

The shock of objective ideas and organic shame are effectively subdued by the conditions of life and addictive behaviors that are clearly related to the "Evil God Self-Calming."

Following the inner and outer mechanical flow of relationships leads to interesting connections. For example, the division of our individual consciousness, and the apparent mirroring of this internal state within society, provide conditions that first reinforce basic egoism and aggression and later help to produce what Gurdjieff calls a Hasnamuss. A Hasnamuss is an empty thing masquerading as a human being, an embodiment of false personality.

Hasnamussian impulses such as "hypocrisy, haughtiness, double-facedness," produce harmful radiations. These impulses are the results of egoistic identification that squash the shock of organic shame leading to the acceptance of addiction as a final means to keep Sacred Conscience from arising. This is the sin that cannot be forgiven.

Returning to the beginning, addictive behavior literally sucks essence dry and strengthens the duality of consciousness by putting the inner part, that is essence, into a deeper sleep.

Since the duality of our consciousness seems to give rise to societal abnormality and both directly and indirectly supports identification, a starting point for change lies in the possibility of attention re-connecting and perhaps eventually erasing this artificially induced duality through the action of consciously receiving impressions. This effort of seeing and feeling my situation can eventually awaken mind and essence to their true relationship.

As this paper begins a little further back in the process, that is, closer to where most of us actually live, it is mainly concerned with behavioral tendencies that re-enforce mechanicalness and may lie at the root of crystallizing into a Hasnamuss. Certain of these tendencies must be eliminated.

If our Work is to survive, we cannot be two-faced; we must find our way back to our one true face, given us before we were born. The other related result, which Gurdjieff pays special attention to in the *Third Series*, must be guarded against as well. We do not want our Work unintentionally to support the creation of "inner double gravity centered existences" to which the duality of consciousness is heir.

On Combining Psychological Energetic Methods to the Problem of Kundabuffer

Gurdjieff took a conservative approach to the elimination of the effects of the Organ Kundabuffer. It was what he recommended and indicated; it was also Buddha's approach, so we must take it very seriously. Gurdjieff emphasized one arm of the cross between psychological and energetic methods to destroy this pernicious influence of the Organ Kundabuffer.

The method of choice was psychological: to bear the unpleasant manifestations of others and thereby produce a friction causing heat that would begin to melt down this barrier to normal perception.

What is this heat? It is not just the lower heat of the blood; it is heat related to emotional energies and Hanbledzoin. When I bear the negative manifestations of others, heat rises in both blood and Hanbledzoin (Prana or Chi). Gurdjieff said Hanbledzoin connects mind and emotions while blood connects emotions and body.

This method Gurdjieff considered slow but more sure. The other method is energetic; it is faster, but more subject to self-delusion.

The first method, combined with the aim to understand myself, brings up the "false I's," negative emotional attitudes, even Chief Feature. All of these have accumulated and grown due to the effects of Kundabuffer (See False Genesis Enneagram). They must also be separated so that essence can grow and an "indestructible I" appear within essence.

Unfortunately, few people fully erase the effects of Kundabuffer because it is such a painstakingly slow and arduous process. Now, one could approach this problem both psychologically and energetically as long as one is still taking the path of understanding and not just the path of ordinary doing. The approach would involve heating the base of the spine with both psychological and energetic exercises.

The energetic approach is connected with the alchemical process of producing heat, sometimes called "TU MO" (See the Pathways of Energy Transformation chapter). Heat can be produced in the body by exercise and heat of a higher level through concentrating on the prana with the mind's intent to raise the heat level.

I want to point out one more important fact: Some people practice bearing the unpleasant manifestations of others like a moral cause and do not focus their intent on the three and one half spirals of the snake choking off the normal transformation of Prana. Therefore, although they are making efforts, their efforts are not directed to where Gurdjieff specifically points, and thus the efforts have little or no effect on Kundabuffer.

Combining these two methods under the umbrella of the aim of Understanding could lead to a more effective method of beginning the process leading to true transformation. The crossing of psychological and energetic practices whose nexus is this Chi or Pranic heat can accelerate the changes we must make in order to begin productive Work on Ourselves. This is the Way of the Sly Man and a synergetic approach to overcoming this first barrier.

Thus the fruits of the tree of Kundabuffer such as false personality and chief feature must also be erased. See Enneagram of False Genesis and in vol. 2 the deconstruction of this enneagram.

NOTES

[1] G. Gurdjieff, *All and Everything, First Series: Beelzebub's Tales to His Grandson* (Aurora, Oregon: Two Rivers Press, 1993), 105.
[2] William Shakespeare, "Macbeth," Act 5, Scene 5

Fear: The Mind Awakener

Fear. What is it? Why do I become so afraid? These questions haunted me when I was very young. It was a strange process from childhood. Childhood trauma notwithstanding, I felt it was wrong to be so afraid. From very early in life I was curious about fear, annoyed at how it controlled me at times: hiding under covers, from both real and imagined fears, not wanting to go into dark rooms at night.

While still a young boy, I began experiments with myself and with seeing fear as a foe. I walked into the back bedroom alone in the dark, or with my eyes closed. Sometimes I walked in darkness backwards all the way and into the closet, testing fear against rationality, in a safe environment. It seemed there was at the same time a stronger sense both of myself and of my environment, which I did not constate but felt; so it intrigued me.

Later as a teenager and young man, I would sometimes walk through dark alleys in Los Angeles; I began to be more and more fascinated by the increase of sensory awareness, of small events that I would not have noticed otherwise: sounds, for example; and minute sounds.

Sometimes I would hitch hike up through northern California and stay alone in the forest, at times with very strange things happening around me. It was at this time that I became sure that fear could be an ally to enhance awareness, and even a doorway to higher perceptions. So I was interested in further testing this: I would walk amongst swarms of bees and become totally immersed in their vibratory world.

One day I was walking on a trail, and I saw a rattlesnake in front of me. The thought came to me that someone might come down this trail in a jeep and run him over. So I began to speak to this snake and picked him up in my hands. I continued to speak to him and brought him to a safer place.

Many other experiments with fear were to follow (see "Facts"), some very powerful. I came to realize that fear was created for the enhancement of awareness and attention in dangerous situations, and one need not diminish one's capacity to respond. One can greatly increase not only the perception of reality but also the ability to handle any situation better.

It became clear: this is a door that swings both ways, and it is our choice once we have become clear about fear's true function, to either lose our self in fear or become connected with higher centers and greater degrees of freedom.

Moscow Webinar on Tension, False I, Breathing, and Higher Being Bodies

We could talk about a few things, and I would appreciate all your questions or observations.

One of the things we spoke about in the title of the program was the relationship between certain tensions in our body that are connected with, or making concrete, the False I. Therefore the tension can give clues as to where and what this False I is.

Our body can have tensions that drain us and correct tensions that support us. While we are talking about this tonight you can also be observing yourself and observing the tensions in your body. In this way you can begin to develop an approach to reducing these false tensions and the False I that is connected to it.

If you observe little children, you can see that the way they move, the way their postures are, the way their facial expressions are: all are more fluid. The energy or prana flows through them more easily than through us. As we grow older we begin to lose this flexibility, this fluidity. If you lose this fluidity, you begin to become more rigid, and that rigidity is psychological as well as physical.

The other part of the subject that we want to talk about tonight is the energetic aspect, which is connected with prana or chi, and how we can gradually develop what Gurdjieff calls "higher bodies." The physical aspect, like this inner circle here (draws a diagram; see below), the lowest aspect, as you are going down through the Ray of Creation, has to be understood, but also the mind has to be understood.

In previous seminars we have talked about what I have termed to be three barriers. The first barrier we spoke about is in the physical body. Gurdjieff calls it "Kundabuffer." This aspect turns impressions upside down in the sense of valuation, so that you begin to value outer life, outer things, more than inner things. So, this first barrier is connected with the very base of the spine.

The second barrier is in the medulla oblongata, and this is right in the top of the spinal nerves. This is the place—Gurdjieff speaks about—where the results of your efforts can be turned into their opposites.[1] Gurdjieff also speaks about this barrier as the place of the crossing between the left and right sides of the body, in the brain.

I am calling these "barriers" because they are barriers to transformation. There is dysfunction here creating this barrier, between the left and right side of the brain. A neutralizing force must come, a reconciling force. If this third force can come, then these two sides can work together.

The third barrier is that the emotional center has been divided into two parts: one is the heart, and the other is the solar plexus. The solar plexus is connected more with the body and the sympathetic nervous system. The heart is a very powerful electrical organ; we know that electricity is connected with the idea of the "spirit" and "consciousness." The relationship between the higher (heart) and lower (solar plexus) parts of ourselves must begin to be integrated in order to start dissolving this third barrier which has formed.

So, with regard to the mind and the "I": the "I" that can exist for us now, is simply "my attention." If my attention is held, is enslaved through identification, then my "I" is simply a part of the many "I's." That is, there is no one I; there are I's. I can create a kind of separation, an independence for my attention.

Therefore, using my attention, I have to work with non-identification. I have to be able to separate my mind from the reactions that occur in my life, set my mind apart from likes and dislikes. Gradually then, if I can do this, I can create a kind of separation, or independence from my attention. Then this attention will have become two forces, one looking inward and one looking outward.

As I look around me, I can be aware of people and surroundings, and I can be aware of my inner state, but without judgment. As soon as I see judgment come in, then I am identified. If I am identified, and I go into these little parts of myself, this is fragmentation. So I want to step aside from this identification.

In his symbol of Akhaldan, Gurdjieff uses the substance of amber to represent the capacity to non-identify or to be impartial. Also in this statue you have the three parts of the system.

You have first the body and what Gurdjieff calls "perseverance"; that is, you do not stop; you keep going; this idea is represented by the Bull.

Then you have the emotions, and here the major quality you need is courage, courage to face yourself, to face your life. Courage, in the Akhaldan statue, is symbolized by the Lion.

And finally you have the mind, or the intellect. And the mind must constantly keep some Aim. So that if you are working for example, with attention now, with this process of being connected at the same time with the inside of yourself as well as the outside, at the same moment, then the Aim is that this third force is going to enter, that you will be open to this third force, which will relate these two parts of yourself, the inner and the outer. So they are no longer separate; they are now becoming integrated. And this integration means that you are developing your own individuality, your own Real I.

So here you have in this symbol, the eagle represents the freedom of the mind, the freedom of attention so that, as the eagle's wings go up, it flies above and it can look down on things; through this analogy you can see the whole of yourself, the whole of the situation. So, in order to counter-balance the barriers, you have to develop these qualities.[2]

And then, a very strange situation is occurring in the statue, where, instead of having a head on the figure, you have the piece of amber where the neck is, and you have the breasts of a virgin, which represent giving love. Here is the idea of non-identification. For most of us, what we call love, is simply identification. It is involved with our likes and our dislikes, but this love is something more than that: this love is something that you have to pass, through non-identification, in order to get to. And when you do, maybe then you can, really give. Potentially there is the possibility of some love that is not egoistic, that comes from the whole of myself, all three centers. With this, we begin to bring together our three parts into a kind of harmony. But if we try to force our parts together, then we are going to get a kind of disharmony.

So, we see that the mind must be clear. So if you are here in this room now, and you can have your mind absolutely clear, then you can see what is going on in yourself, and you can begin to take in new ideas directly. As we are, our ordinary mind does not take in new ideas directly, because there is no active element in us. And if this active element is not there when the mind is taking in an impression, then this impression gets diverted into what Gurdjieff calls "formatory apparatus," which is simply a means to label things, sort of like a librarian who labels things.

One of the main exercises for us is not to be overloaded with associations. Associations are there; they are helpful; they are needed, but you should not be enslaved to associations. You should be able to take things out of the library and work with them, but, in a sense, not have all the books fall on your head. We want to make use of formatory apparatus, rather than let it make use of us. That means we must have some control over our own attention. So, I am looking at this, I am looking at the words, and I am trying to keep my mind open.

Down below we have Kundabuffer, and we remember that the main way Gurdjieff talks about dissolving Kundabuffer is through working with other people. It is not the only way, which we will talk about perhaps another time. To address Gurdjieff's main way: if somebody irritates you, if perhaps they judge you, and you see they are judging you, in order to Work, you have to bear this unpleasant judgment, for example, from another person. By bearing it, inner friction is created inside of you. This has an effect on your self-image and on the tensions in your body that we were talking about, the tensions that create the False I. Now ordinarily, if somebody says something that affects your self-image, you find some way to protect it, and it seems that you are protecting yourself. But you are not; you are protecting this False I. That is why this quality of courage is so necessary: so that when you see that this false image is being attacked, or you feel that it is being attacked, you don't turn away. You face yourself, not because the person is necessarily right or good, but because you want to dissolve this False I.

As far as emotional life is concerned, how do I not go with my emotional reactions? How do I keep back? How can I be patient? This builds a certain emotional strength, but if it is in the form of suppression, then I am going to create greater dysfunction. So, how can I bring my emotions, which Gurdjieff links to the idea of the horse, how can I bring my emotional life to support my Aim?

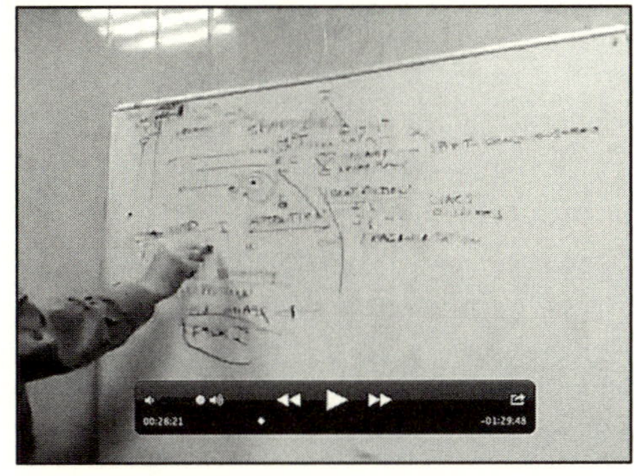

Do any of you have an idea? How do you convince your animal not to react with anger? For example: How do I convince the horse that it is better not to react? (There is much discussion in audience.) Let's say you are a person who likes to lecture, so you begin to lecture your horse about how great it would be if he did not react. Would that help? (Someone in audience suggests stories in childhood.) So one way is through stories; that is how we help children to understand—fairy tales, mythology. And it used to be common throughout the world that stories were told in groups of people, even large groups of people.

So, if the driver, the mind—and you remember that the mind has many parts, but let's say three parts: the part related to the moving center, the part related to the emotional center, the part related to the thinking center. One has to be able to move into this emotional part of the mind in order to have rapport with the emotional center. If the mind is so objectified that it has no connection with life, then it cannot connect with emotional center; that is, if it is so objective, in the sense of being almost sterile and isn't connected with life. In this case the mind cannot relate to emotions, or to the body; it can't relate to Being.

Remember, the evolution comes from the higher, entering into the lower, creating the moving, instinctive, and sexual centers and then creating the emotional center and then the intellectual center. And if the intellectual center is going to relate to these two lower centers, there has to be some kind of related component.

In the brain itself there are these components so that the intellectual center is not separated from the being, from the emotions, and the body. But on the other hand, if you never work with the emotional part of the intellectual center or the moving part of the intellectual center, you don't have this relationship. So, if you're telling a myth, which involves the intellectual center, ideas, concepts, you're making a connection, creating a rapport.

And you are creating a support for your emotional life. And, in the myth, one is shown how to take steps towards a better life, towards a more whole life. And one is also warned about different struggles which may arise, difficulties to be faced, so the horse is prepared for difficulties. Also the horse is motivated by the fact that, as these steps are taken, gradually one become stronger and lives in a higher state of being. So the horse can be motivated, not just by this way, but this is one of the ways.

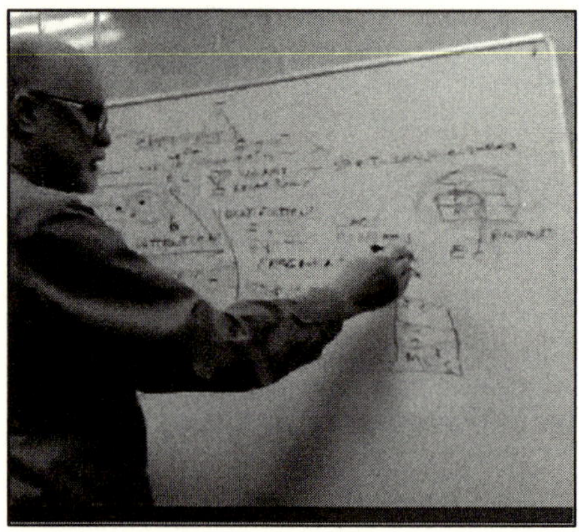

As you may remember, Mr. Gurdjieff tells us that myth connects, not only with emotional center but with Higher Emotional Center. So here again the emotional center is supported by being connected with the higher part of itself. When impressions come in, and they are connected with Higher Emotional Center, then you get these very alive impressions of yourself and of the world. This involves mystical states. So now the horse really has something to look forward to. In essence, the horse gets wings. So now the horse is free from many, many of its old neuroses, fears, anxiety, stresses because it sees that there is a whole other purpose to life. And it can come to this higher purpose by following these steps.

Now, have any of you been watching your tensions at all? Your postures? It's easy to forget your aim—if it's your aim. Maybe you had a different aim. If you had a different aim, were you following that? But it's easy to be side-tracked; you could have interesting ideas, or you could have a TV show, an interesting party—and you forget your aim. If you don't have an aim, you cannot have an "I."

I remember, Lord Pentland said, "All we have is attention." But if the attention is not connected to an aim, it is equally useless.

What is that old saying? If you don't know where you are going, any port is good enough. (From a person in audience: In Russian the saying is, nobody can make us choose the wrong way because we don't have any.) (Then, a lot of audience participation, sharing). Yes. From our point of view you can go nowhere. You go in a Magic Circle, what Ouspensky spoke about as repetition. You repeat and repeat. So, at some point in this process, it may be that you get help from the outside. But then you have to educate the body, the horse, and the mind, each one; otherwise you very soon come back to this circle.

And this circle is held, partly, by the tensions in your body. So, while we're talking about it, you are going to make the attempt to let go of the common tension in your body. I always liked that idea that Carlos Castenada had—he had some brilliant ideas—and he was talking about, the fact that at a certain place in your body, everything is held together, and if something hits it (AF pops one fist into palm of the other open and cupped hand), you can displace that. (Lots of audience participation during translation.) Then, it becomes more fluid, temporarily. So you can observe and watch, perhaps you have an area in your body on which these tensions focus or vector. And how would it be if you released this false center of gravity? Maybe you can find for yourself where the tensions focus or vector in your body. For some people it's very obvious; they will be like this: (AF tenses his upper body including raised shoulders). You can just feel this pressure and this tension; they get headaches. And this is like holding up the world sort of thing.

So you want to find for yourself where these tensions tend to gravitate. It could be in your body; it could be in your head. In a lot of people it is in the base of your spine, where you are supposed to have a tail. We lost our tail (there was one actually, when you were an embryo; in the embryo there is actually a primitive tail). In some rare cases, people actually grow a tail. So, it is still there in our DNA. It is very interesting; at the base of the spine, here was the tail (makes drawing). When you have a dog, for example, it will bring its tail around like this (makes "C" shape figure from Kundabuffer spot) when it has fear. And, if you are watching, you will find that this can happen also to you; that is, you will find the base of the spine curving, tensing. And so when you are in a state of fear, this part, which is connected to Kundabuffer here, pulls your energy in like this (tenses upper torso, hands inwards).

So what happens when you try to consciously relax this part (at base of your spine)? It has an effect on the whole body because this reaction is connected with the adrenalin flow and the lack of ability to absorb this neurohormone in the right way.

In all these many different places you might have these tensions, whether it's in the chest or whether it's in the lower back, or it could even be in the legs, anywhere; if you begin to consciously release the tightness, try to see what you are releasing. It may not be something you can label intellectually, but you can kind of take a picture of it: what is this tension? What is it related to?

You know you can be watching the scary movie, or reading a book that has some scary theme, and in your head, you can say to yourself, "This is just a movie." But you can see that you are not able to persuade your instinctive center, or your emotional center, of the truth of that. Even though it's just a movie, and you know it can't hurt you, or it's a kind of dream, you see that illusion is stronger than your mind. But gradually, if you work with the tensions that are created by this illusion, then the illusion also begins to disappear. And this is another way of helping to dissolve Kundabuffer.

Kundabuffer is creating these illusionary states, what they call in Hinduism, "Maya." Remember Buddha was sitting under the tree and he was attacked by Maya. And so we each are going to be in the position of being attacked in a sense by Maya, of something that is taking our life force, our prana. Gurdjieff calls that life force "hanbledzoin,"and in Taoism it's "Qi." They are just different names for the same substance.

So if you want to have more life energy, you have to reduce the amount of this energy being taken away. Did anybody find a place in themselves where there is this concentration of tension? (Audience participation: "calves") Yes, the calves, absolutely, that can be a place of tensing. It is interesting, because children get a lot of calf spasms.

Pain is also an indicator of dysfunction.

(From audience: How can you change from negative to positive tension in your body?) The way you can find out is by experimentation. For example, you are sitting there and maybe you have a certain tension in your body; ask yourself, do you need it? Is it helping? Try to let go, and see if you need it. If you relax too much, you fall asleep. So there is a certain amount of tension that is necessary for the body to be in a posture. There might be a certain amount of tension necessary for you to stay awake. But if you hold on very tightly, then you are simply going to lose energy because tension requires energy.

What would it be like if the only tension you expended was enough to stay in the place that you are in, nothing more; you are so efficient? And it may be that different postures bring out certain states, like somebody may be in a posture where they have their hand like this (not visible) or something–the famous posture "the Thinker." Does it help you think? You have to see. Maybe it does.

And in Sitting positions, when you are trying to meditate, is there a particular posture that helps you meditate? Probably if you are like this (stiffens and raises shoulders), it doesn't help. But it takes time to allow yourself to come into a new posture. You know, what's this posture (arms crossed over chest)? Like Sitting Bull, the American Indian. It can be a very strong posture. It depends upon what state you are trying to bring out.

(Someone in audience: "Let's take a break.") Good idea.

We have been speaking about the body that can have tensions that drain us, and correct tensions that support us. You can say the latter are "mechanically efficient" tensions; that is, they are not mechanical in the negative sense but in the positive sense. Then, there are tensions which are unnecessary and are connected with a kind of false way to face your life, you might say. I may have in my mind that I have to be a certain way, and I don't question it. For example, you are some big guy, and you see yourself as always having to be very tough, always. Or, you always have to be very theatrical. Or intellectual: you are always thinking. You may not be thinking, but you are always pretending you are thinking. You create these postures which are false, which require these tensions which are false, and these tensions support False I, like the base of a pyramid. If you begin to take away the base of false postures and tensions, gradually you begin to reduce the development of this False I.

On the other side, you have natural tensions, normal tensions, healthy tensions, that support the development of your Real I.

What do these normal tensions do? They allow for prana to flow. It is prana that feeds essence and allows Real I to grow. You can't grow, psychologically, this Real I without sufficient Life Force.

Now you see that mind and body are going to be connected through this energy, this prana. It is a linking ground, connecting between mind and body. In order for this prana to be strong, you have to have the correct breath. If you want your mind and body to relate properly to each other, you have to begin to learn to breathe properly. But, because of the false tensions, because of this False I that has developed, my breath is attenuated. So I am not breathing naturally, and my prana, my life force, is reduced. Therefore this connection between mind and body, and body, mind, emotions is cut off.

You may see that in the Gurdjieff Foundation, there is some fear concerning "breathing exercises." That is because Gurdjieff warned us that certain artificial types of breathing can be harmful. And so this kind of anxiety or fear of the process has become part of the Foundation, and many people are then afraid to work with breathing.

And so, the life force, which we need and which Gurdjieff calls "Hanbledzoin,"is not strengthened. If it is not strengthened, you cannot create Higher Being Bodies. So, you stay with this physical body, this planetary body, and that's all you'll have. Therefore, it is absolutely necessary to understand breathing, and the first step is to reestablish your natural, free flowing breath.

These tensions that we have, these false tensions, are connected with anxiety, emotional stress, and can even be connected with psychosis. When the normal flow of energy, the normal life force, is aberrated, you can get illness in the body, in the emotions, and in the mind.

Gurdjieff said that if you don't deal with these dysfunctions, you cannot have any kind of productive Work. Therefore, he said that some people needed to be trained in healing in these three areas, in order that these dysfunctions can be dissolved, and one can begin to live more naturally. When you begin to live and breathe and think more naturally, then you are supporting the growth of essence, that is, who you are, (who I am).

So you have to deal to some extent with these disease states, or imbalanced states, at the same time that you are working on developing your true self. And, through this process of mind and body now working in harmony together, more and more of this prana, and higher prana, that is, higher hydrogens, are drawn in, and this in turn brings essence up, and finally at the top of the pyramid, Real I is created.

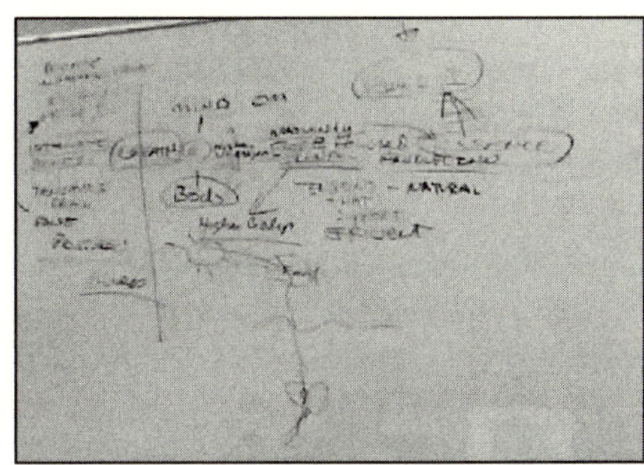

It is like the lotus that gradually grows up through the muddy water (AF draws plant with root submerged, and at surface of water, flower stem blooming), and here is the sun; these are higher hydrogens. The lotus can get these higher energies, and inside you have the real human being, or the pearl in the lotus. So this lotus is an image in ancient Egypt, in India and in China, and other places to illustrate the idea of evolution. Flowers have been used as a part of the language that supports this idea.

So, you see that all this is critical to our possible evolution. And it is interesting that a number of people in the Gurdjieff Work have studied Tai Chi and Xi Gong, Alexander Technique, Feldenkrais, and other kinds of methods in order to bring these techniques to people. Michel de Salzmann worked a lot with voice, with singing; so did Gurdjieff. And when you work with voice, and work with singing, you are working with breath. So it is an interesting, indirect way to approach.

Now, on hydrogen 48: In relation to the mind, we know that hydrogen 48 is the beginning of the Do of Impressions. We know that hydrogen 48 in the form of Mi 48 is the place where the interval is, in the octave of air. Do 48 and Mi 48 are stuck at this point as we have talked about. Instead of an impression entering deeper and being digested, becoming a Re 24 and Mi 12, for most people, it stays here at Do 48 and is diverted by formatory apparatus. And finally in connection with the body, when you have the digestion of food: where you take in the impression of air, air is digesting, going Do, Re, Mi and it stops. But if I am aware, if I feel my-self, breathing, I am taking in the impression of air intentionally; if I intentionally take in the impression of air, then the octave continues: Do, Re, Mi, Fa 24, Sol 12—all of a sudden I am at this higher level, connected with the Sun. And I know that if I take in the impression by bringing the carbon 12 here, then instead of formatory apparatus slaving this energy, it continues so that it is Do, Re, Mi 12. So in the body I now have this new level of energy, not just to strengthen this carnal body, but for the Astral body and for the Mental body, and to create connection to Higher Emotional Center I now have the appropriate energies.

That is basically what I wanted to cover tonight. Are there any questions?

#1Q: I create energy, prana, but I lose it it; it just disappears. Why?

A: As you make efforts, the False I has a different agenda. As you make efforts to dissolve these barriers, then you are going to be losing less of your energies.

#2Q: If we are lucky and we dissolve the barriers, then how to direct it?

A: It is an alchemical process. It is not automatic; we need very clear formulations and practices to do this, but you begin by working on developing the process we have talked about tonight. You begin by working to put energy into the body; in general, a certain amount stays there in the body; you don't lose it.

#3Q: How is Astral body felt?

A: It is best to read mystical accounts or shamanic accounts. To move this energy out of your body, you might do Tai Chi practices.

We are out of time.

NOTES

[1] G. I. Gurdjieff, *All and Everything, First Series: Beelzebub's Tales to His Grandson* (New York: E.B. Dutton, 1950), p. 791.

[2] Ibid, 311-12.

The Three Fundamental Barriers

Introduction

There are three barriers[1] on the stairway leading to the Fourth Way; many in the Work do not know of these barriers although Gurdjieff speaks of them quite plainly. These are not abstract barriers but concrete ones that exist in the body. In this essay, we begin to address ourselves to these barriers, for these are connected with the false genesis. (See chapter on "False Genesis Enneagram.")

It is interesting to visualize how the hierarchy of centers in the body corresponds exactly to the cosmic hierarchy as Gurdjieff speaks about in BEELZEBUB'S TALES. The true mind exists deep in the brain which sits upon the body which holds in itself the image of the cosmic scheme.

Briefly, moving down from the brain and the power to speak, the throat and down to the heart and then solar plexus, we come to the gut brain in the lower abdomen that is connected to the moving center. The whole is connected via the nervous system (and at another level the pranic or qi channels) as the body is the containment vessel for all and everything.

So when you are sitting or standing, you are a mirror on the Earth for the Ray of Creation. However, when you lie down, it is to sleep. So you are also putting this ladder down. In this position it no longer functions as a stairway to the stars.

Lack of knowledge and understanding of the concept of three barriers prevents our Work from coming to a positive, concrete result. The concept involves three mechanisms that effectively block or aberrate our life energy. Although they appear on the vertical axis within our body, an axis that has been likened to a main pipeline or, better, a conduit, for energy, these barriers influence all the general and sacred channels that distribute life energy and control the functions of the whole body. In addition to the physiological effects, there are also psychological effects that must be understood if one is to evolve conscious Will and a permanent I. In this process one must also rid oneself of the illusions, projections, and domination of the false I, otherwise known as the crystallization of chief feature.

The First Barrier

In his writings Gurdjieff gives much serious attention to the first of these barriers: that is, the effects of the organ Kundabuffer at the base of the spine, where genetically our tail should be. It is the place where animals express their instinctive emotions such as fear and aggression as well as their subjectivity. This subjectivity can be seen for example in a dog wagging its tail or in a cat showing annoyance in flicking its tail, and in more subtle expressions. If you have been an astute observer of the effects of emotion on your physical body, you may have observed micro-movements of your own tailbone under conditions of stress.

Here, according to Mr. Gurdjieff and also, for certain Taoist Masters and Patanjali, there exists something like 3 1/2 rings, or coils of a snake around the base of the lingam. It is a kind of trap that occludes prana or chi or ruach, whatever one wishes to call it—it is the life force. This trap prevents the life force from taking its natural course. In doing so, it causes human beings to see things "topsy-turvy" or "upside down."[2] So, for example, the false I is taken for the real I. (See the chapter on "False Genesis Enneagram.") And the material world is placed in value above the spiritual world. We do not sell all for the pearl of great price; rather we sell our inheritance, our birthright, for a mess of porridge.

This first barrier prevents what Ouspensky called the Psychology of Man's Possible Evolution. Gurdjieff tells us, and we can verify this through observation, that there is something hidden in us that must be dissolved if we are to have any productive Work aimed at self-transformation. (For a fuller exposition, see essay Seeker and Addiction in this book.)

So the suggestion was given to dissolve this "parasite" by enduring the unpleasant manifestation of others: to put oneself—or have oneself put—in conditions that cause suffering, especially to our vanity and pride, to our self-image, and to our sense of what is right, etc. In doing so, over considerable time, the vestiges of Kundabuffer will be eradicated.

There is gross ignorance in those who speak, in a kind of mechanical mantra, about the idea of not Working for a result. This idea was clearly meant to help people think and not as dogma. So, one can see the action of Kundabuffer here. Instead of pondering, people repeated like monkeys, and this gave rise to the original expression, "monkey mind."

As was suggested by Bennett, it may be that Kundabuffer was the reason for the strange insertion of Neanderthal Man in the evolutionary process. Then, when Kundabuffer was being erased from our genetic code, Homo sapiens re-arose. In any case, it is rare to see anyone understand what result we are looking to obtain from the extremely difficult task of transforming the negative forces arising from working with others. And if the aim, the objective, is forgotten, then the octave of effort is wasted, turned aside.

So one needs to have a clear aim and envisioned result, or there is no use making an effort. This envisioned result, however, is based in the Law of Three and the Law of Sevenfoldness. Then one can come to an understanding of what the idea of "not working for a result" might actually mean. Then perhaps one can begin to understand what Gurdjieff is trying to express in the phrase that "man cannot do" while he also tells us that "the highest aim of Man is to be able to do." Try to ponder this; it is not enough to read it or mouth the words.

To do is to incorporate those two fundamental laws in one's life in order to be; to know; to understand. So it is clear that the lack of focus and intention precisely on dissolving the results of Kundabuffer means you will get nowhere.

There may be methods to accelerate the dissolving of Kundabuffer, and we will talk about this at another place in this book (see Handbook on Energy Pathways).

The Second Barrier

There is a movement up the central channel, from the base of spine and instinctive sexual forces towards the second being brain, which is the emotional center.

The next barrier is spoken about by Mr. Gurdjieff, as a kind of cleavage of the emotional center. Whereas at one time this center was unified, for some reason, it was divided into two parts so that in us we have the heart itself and the solar plexus.[3]

Often we do not feel at all; we only emote. Our feelings and our emotions are mechanical, touched off by fear of exposure. Our essential self is hidden and, like a child kept in a closet, cannot manifest its true self.

The solar plexus is connected to the sympathetic nervous system; it is manipulated by fears and hormones which in turn stimulate equally mechanical reactions. Physically or emotionally, if one is hit in the solar plexus, the shock is overwhelming. Many nerves connect from the thoracic spine to the solar plexus. In ancient Egypt and China it was known that if the vertebrae of a person were out of place, he or she would suffer emotional distress mechanically. So here is an example of how our emotions, so highly regarded by us, are often the result of something as innocuous as an out of place vertebrae!

The heart is a highly electrical organ that is given its impetus through the AV node and runs down into the center via the Purkinje fibers. Electricity and magnetism, which are much greater than the output of our mechanical brain (because we hardly use it), are the stuff of the higher emotional center.

The arterial blood (H48) has at its center iron which has a positive charge and magnetically attracts oxygen with its negative charge. The electrical energy of the heart is distributed to the body through the blood and its salts. The heart has been shown to communicate to the head brain, and it is clear that through the blood, its energy and hormones, it communicates to the body as well. Blood, according to Gurdjieff, links the horse to the carriage—the emotional center to the moving center, which is housed in the spinal cord and lowest part of the brain, about which we will say more a little later.

Intuition and awareness are qualities of higher emotional center, while proximity awareness is a function of the solar plexus. We must reunite the two parts of the emotional center through body/feeling exercises. (See the exercises in this book.) Intuition and awareness are related to the conscious connection to the blood and hormones, one of the main linkages being adrenaline and other neural hormones. The reader can study this topic further in standard physiology texts.

The heart—what is it? In order to understand, one must awaken. One must be willing to suffer, to open and give of oneself so that the process of moving from Sol - Do is understood and so that the purpose of organic life is completed.

The Third Barrier

The third barrier is the crossing of neurological impulses in the back and lower part of the head brain, called the medulla oblongata. In speaking about it Gurdjieff says concerning this vital crossing of two forces arising up from the whole body, both left and right sides, that one must be vigilant and attentive: "very, very much on guard" (i.e., vigilant and attentive) or this will give "results not similar but 'opposite to each other'." And, he says, "That is why, in respect of these being-substances, the beings themselves must always be very, very much on their guard in order to avoid undesirable consequences for their entire whole."[4]

Again, I repeat: "very, very much on guard" (i.e., vigilant and attentive) or this will give "results not similar but opposite to each other." The crossing of these forces without a reconciling or third force can create only artificial electricity that drains us of the power to transform ourselves. This is why—and try to ponder this—the force of attention guided by understanding is vital at this third barrier.

The medulla oblongata stands between the planetary body, as it is contiguous with the spinal cord, and the higher centers in the brain. In deep Taoist teachings this area is called the "Jade Pillow" because it is where sleep is induced; connect this to what was said before. It has a controlling influence on the cardiac, respiratory, and many reflex functions such as coughing, sneezing, swallowing, vomiting as well as heart rate, and blood pressure.

The medulla oblongata also controls fine motor activity such as writing and even speech and turning of the head. (In Parkinson's disease this finer motor function is attenuated.) By paying closer attention, you can follow back these activities towards their source in the medulla. It detects excess acid in blood through chemo-receptors and tells the lungs to increase oxygen supply. So you can see that oversight and reconciling this crossing is crucial to our Work, and yet no one speaks of it, except, of course, Gurdjieff himself. We must go much deeper into sensation in these three places: the base of the spine, the chest, and the "back of the head" where this crossing of forces actually occurs. (See "Handbook on Energy Pathways.")

The latter barrier is connected with the disharmony between male and female elements. Male and female logic and intuition should potentiate each other, but they rarely do. Before it turns into seed, the creative force strengthens our ability on one side towards scientific investigation and on the other towards artistic pursuits. Yet a whole human being, as an ideal like Leonardo Da Vinci, would balance these two attributes and not be isolated in one or the other.

The question may arise in those who seriously study, how do these three barriers relate to other aspects of our Work such as the problem of Formatory Apparatus? It is an apparatus which should act as a support for thinking and reason, a kind of librarian with access to memory and associations that can be brought forward easily and examined. However, instead of being a useful tool, it usurps and replaces our highest function, thought. So, instead of thought, we are trapped in this automatism, the Monkey Mind, as our default mode, which in turn is enslaved to our fantasies and illusions.

Summary

The first barrier is a labyrinth of illusion that holds onto and sucks out our prana or higher hydrogens that are prerequisites for the first conscious shock. These are needed to digest impressions. This can only come about if these substances are first diverted away from formatory apparatus so that they continue their natural and purposeful evolution.

The second barrier causes emotional disharmony and negative states, even hysteria.

The third barrier polarizes but does not reconcile the rising neurological inputs to the brain from the body, impulses already negatively influenced by the two lower barriers. As they cross and enter the brain at the medulla oblongata, this confusion influences the sympathetic and parasympathetic systems. And in addition to all the physiological processes, the impressions coming in are not met with the necessary higher energy C12, as only a conscious intention can overcome the dysfunctional effects of these three barriers.[5]

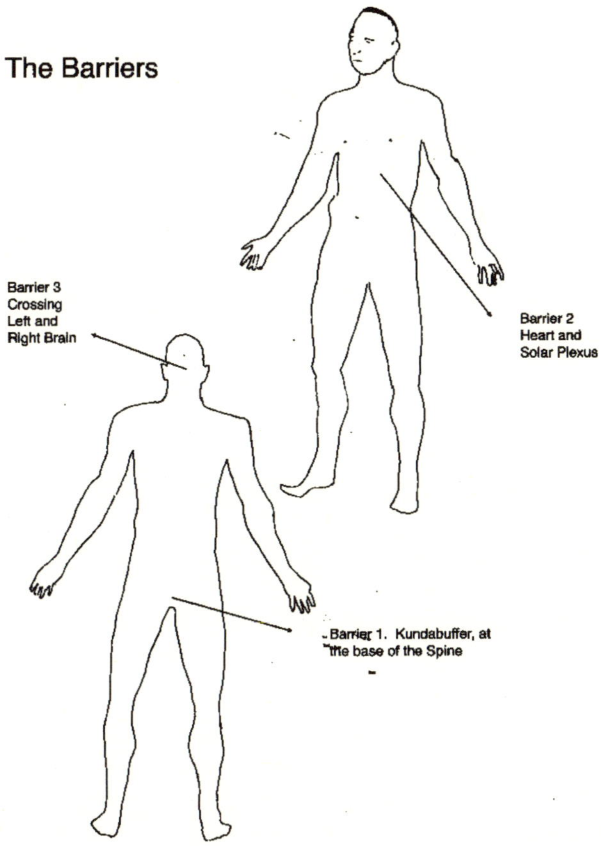

Under these conditions, in addition to the natural forces that oppose evolution, it becomes clearer why so few are "chosen" to evolve. In fact few even see through these barriers; even the instinctive desire for self-perfection has been lost, Gurdjieff tells us.

If we do not see what is preventing the initiation of our metamorphosis, we cannot begin to free ourselves from these traps. These traps effectively stop us from taking even these first steps on the evolutionary ladder.

So now we have some idea of what we are up against and why many people in our Work get nowhere. The tree of knowledge shows those who can see, where to find the tree of life and where upon the tree of life the fruit of eternal life will appear, where the branching appears and life erupts from the branch.

This Work is exacting; one must discover precisely how to look. One must become a detective, a hunter poised, listening, to uncover what is true and what is not. One must be focused like a wolf—pointed ears; sheep cannot do this.

NOTES

[1] These Three Fundamental Barriers are to be distinguished from the barriers Gurdjieff speaks of related to tasks and chief feature on pp. 228-231 of P.D. Ouspensky's *In Search of the Miraculous* (New York: Harcourt, Brace, and Co. 1949).

[2] G. I. Gurdjieff, *All and Everything, First Series: Beelzebub's Tales to His Grandson* (New York: E.B. Dutton, 1950), p. 88.

[3] Ibid, 779-780.

[4] Ibid, 791.

[5] The same substances evolving towards the higher sexual hormones from the food we eat—are derived from the intake of air and impressions.

A Walk along the Water:

A Teaching Story and Dialogue with a Pupil

The Story
From the Egyptian

In times past, precious metals were made into ingots and talents: lead, copper, silver, and gold were cast and formed to be used for exchange. In addition, certain amalgams that were more precious than gold, including Orichalc, a reddish gold amalgam-said to shimmer like fire, were created by Egyptian alchemists.

When the Master walked the Earth, he gave to each of his disciples a talent of precious metal to be used for their development, that is, to be invested. These disciples were called the Master's servants.

Then the Master went on a long journey into the mountains where they could not follow. And his servants, with their investiture, were left to do good with what the Master had given them.

After a time, without notice, suddenly the Master appeared among them, and he asked for an accounting.

Some of his servants had used what was given wisely and had completed their purpose on the Earth plane, having turned one talent of gold into ten. To them even more was given; in fact, the Master gave them double (the meaning of which was clear). It is just as when it is told "cast your bread upon the waters." For those who have ears let them hear.

Still others were able to return five talents of gold, and with this, they were given five more, and they came to rest at the place of sacrifice and transmutation. In Egypt a temple was maintained for this purpose. It was from this temple that they were given the means to continue on their journey, the road to inner development.

Then there were the many who, for one reason or another, either because they were fearful of change, or because they were lazy thieves, or for whatever the reason, they were startled by the Master's sudden appearance. They returned the one talent given to them. And the Master said to these latter, "You are neither hot nor cold, so I spew you from my mouth." And then he said to them, "Even that which you have shall be taken from you. The law is exacting and without sentimentality. You have invoked it to your own fault, and now your sin cannot be forgiven."

On the seventh day the Master said, "The harvest is great, but there be but a few in the field to gather it up." And those who had put their hand to the plow, but did not fulfill their task, fell from the Earth plane to where there shall be weeping and gnashing of teeth.

◊◊◊

And at that same time, not far away, the false King was being seduced by the temple dancers, even Salome, who would have revenge upon the prophet John, from the White Brotherhood. He was the one, the I, crying out in the wilderness; in the desert he had prophesized the witch's end, and she would have his death.

And there was a great feast, and Salome with her followers danced, and the false King, who had made promises to her, was forced to fulfill them. So, upon a platter the prophet's head appeared. It was given to the dancers. Then, with arms raised, hands high in the air, holding it aloft above their heads, in celebration and ecstasy, they passed the platter around as they danced their dances, laughing and shouting. Salome had won, and they drank and ate and made merry.

But then, suddenly, the mouth of the prophet opened, and John began to prophesize that the witch, the false King, and the temple would fall, and a true King would arise. Then all was silent and frozen.

The curtain came down on the last act of "The False King and the Witch," and the sun began to rise, coppery gold upon the horizon.

Amun Ra
This is the testament of the Egyptian, the alchemist.

The Dialogue

Cs: All right.

Af: So that is enough for now.

Af: You can comment.

Cs: It is powerful.

Af: You understand the law of octaves.

Cs: Yes.

Af: The doubling brings one up a level. The double is also name for second body—so when the double is given there is revealed the divine essence.

Cs: No, I did not understand that. Maybe it could be added.

Af: Yes I want people to have to think. That is why I say "the meaning of which is clear." That is why I add, "Cast your bread upon the waters." It is a Do. The waters ripple, vibrate, and can return to Do, but higher."

Af: The ocean is a place of endless power. To cast into ocean is to cast upon the great powers, like a prayer, you see.

Cs: Yes.

Af: You give away but are returned 7 fold; fold upon fold, building. When God created the world and the waters, the Logos was upon the waters—like breath, and caused it to ripple—to fold upon itself. So "cast bread upon water" is folding one's energy—building upon each effort towards the next octave—"return sevenfold" is the law of sevenfoldness. Gurdjieff speaks about it in BEELZEBUB'S TALES. But it is not just a passive idea; it is a way to work, a method: "I do not just make disconnected efforts; each effort must build upon the other."

The feel of this enfolding sensation, multiplying of energies, is concentrating energy.

Cs: Like ocean wave developing before crest?

Af: Yes, building up.

Af: Bread is body. The astral body is octave higher.

Cs: Yes. I see.

Af: So it is a kind of enfolding. And the creation is a kind of unfolding.

Cs: John's head on platter, when speaking, was from octave higher.

Af: Yes. Power above ordinary body. As it is said, the man is the head, the I, which can live independent of physical body, with astral body, or mental.

Cs: Yes. And this story embodies the concept.

Af: Yes. They strove to kill John, but they liberated him.

Cs: All this needs to be said.

To be continued in Volume II.

False Genesis Enneagram

Outer Circulation

9 Eternal Retribution

0 Kundabuffer (Kundalini) Trapping prana and Impressions

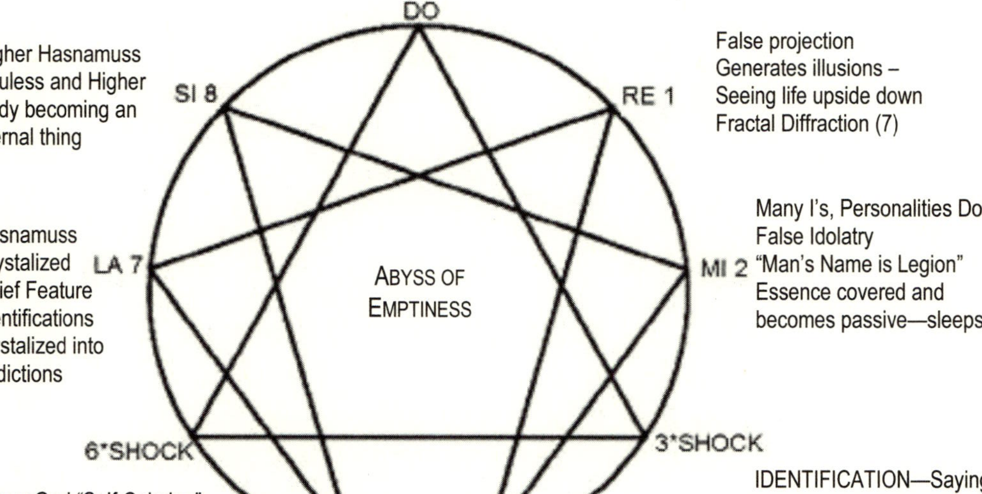

Higher Hasnamuss Souless and Higher Body becoming an eternal thing

Hasnamuss Crystalized Chief Feature Identifications crystalized into addictions

Inner God "Self Calming" Fire from Denial of Truth Fuses (Doppelganger) Buffers Forming

Forming Chief Feature around which all egoism and mechanicality revolve. False Idol begins to take form. A caricature of some essential feature.

False projection
Generates illusions –
Seeing life upside down
Fractal Diffraction (7)

Many I's, Personalities Dominate
False Idolatry
"Man's Name is Legion"
Essence covered and becomes passive—sleeps

IDENTIFICATION—Saying "I"
Monsieur Self Love and
Madame Vanity

Idol picture (egoplastikoori appears)
FALSE PERSONALITY
Belief in what I am not solidifies
Begins to materialize
Roles and Masks

Inner Circulation

1 to 4 Create False Picture of Self

4 to 2 Reinforces projection

2 to 8 Division from True Self begins and culminates

8 to 5 Informs Chief Feature as to this false ideal

5 to 7 Form supporting crystallization

7 to 1 Crystal focuses

"Facts"

My Inner Search for the Gurdjieff Work

"But all the same, you know, the important thing is facts," I said. "If I could see genuine and real facts of a new and unknown character, only they would finally convince me that I am on the right way."

I was again thinking of "miracles."

"There will be facts," said G." I promise you. But many other things are necessary first."

I did not understand his last words then, I only understood them later when I really came up against "facts," for G kept his word. But this was not until about a year and a half later, in August, 1916."

—P.D. Ouspensky, IN SEARCH OF THE MIRACULOUS[1]

Like Ouspensky, I have also felt the necessity to search out such facts, but I have found they come most often on their own terms, preceded by a quiet tug. Animated by a subtle call, my body begins to move, as if it has a will of its own. I begin to wander: I walk about. This story began just that way, when my own search brought me to the miraculous. What appeared then was a fact, an encounter with a super-conscious force.

But I am getting ahead of myself.

I was twenty, and it was the end of a hot summer; more than thirty summers since have come and gone. It was a summer spent working with my friend Cole and several migrant farm workers on the prune harvest at the Barletta Farm in Orland, California. I got up each morning to meditate as the sun rose and to do Tai Chi before leaving for a ten-hour workday.

Living very frugally on a nearby olive orchard, I managed to sock away about $500 dollars for my first trip to Mexico. I went in search of indigenous shamans and Indian sorcerers called Brujos. In a dark green 1956 Volkswagen I took the long journey south through the central desert. I attempted to remember myself as much as possible driving almost non-stop past Mexico City. In this way several times I exhausted all my accumulated energy, and I experienced my first super effort. It was a reckless and dangerous effort, the kind we only make when we are young. With only a few hours rest and little food, I finally found myself in a small village, and there I was told of a gringa in whose house I might stay the night.

It was a few hours before sunset when I pocketed my car key and walked stiffly up to a small adobe hacienda painted pink with blue trim. Exhausted but excited, I dropped off my sleeping bag, and, after making brief acquaintance with the owner of the house, I decided not to rest but to go for a hike. My gracious hostess indicated with a wave of her hand the direction to an Aztec ruin which she said was situated in the low mountains that rose above the eastern edge of the village.

I walked several blocks through the small town, past the small open-air market, where flies vied with locals for slabs of beef and pork. I turned left onto a well-worn dirt road that began a slow rise into the mountains. For reasons still unclear to me, I veered off to the right on to a small, winding footpath partially obscured by thick green foliage. Although I knew I was wandering away from the road I was told to follow, I had no desire to stop and retrace my steps. After about ten minutes I found myself looking up at a sheer granite cliff rising about sixty or seventy feet above the trail. I felt that the ruins might be somewhere above me, so I began to climb.

As I started the ascent, my mind took notice of many things. I was wearing old army boots that were exceptionally clumsy for climbing, and a fair amount of water was streaming down the cliff, making the rocks damp and slippery.

Nevertheless, I made good progress and was soon about two body lengths from the top. My fingers searched for the next handhold but found none. My toes rested on a sliver of rock, and my fingers were contorted claw-like, the tips blanched white trying to maintain a handhold. My attention was focused on my body and the rock face. Time seemed to slow to a stop. I looked down.

Some fifty feet below was the rocky path where I had stood a few minutes ago. If I fell I would be seriously injured or even killed. I looked back up. Keeping my right hand on the rock face, I stretched my left hand as high as I could. Several feet above my grasp was a thick shrub, one of those hardy plants that eke out an existence on solid rock. If I could only reach it, I might pull myself up, but it was too high. It was impossible.

Suspended there, I searched my memory for something, anything, from Taoism, Castaneda, or Gurdjieff that might help. I could not make my way down without falling. I could not reach the only handhold above me, and I was fast losing the strength needed to stay where I was. There was no one around and no one likely to appear. I heard a voice say, "How did I get here?" My fingers were beginning to shake with strain.

A test was in front of me. Was there any truth in these stories of supernatural powers and higher bodies? Was there anything that could help me now?

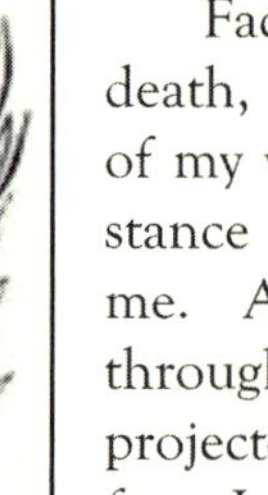

Faced with imminent death, there came a blending of my will with a similar substance in the space around me. A "doorway" opened through which my body was projected vertically by several feet. I was literally transported upward. In the same moment I found my right hand firmly gripping the shrub. Buoyed by the remnants of that force, I easily pulled myself to the top of the cliff.

I slowly stood up and took stock of my surroundings. In this state of extraordinary clarity, there seemed no miracle in what had happened. My ordinary mind, tethered to a different reality, was struck dumb.

I looked around. To my left there was a stone well, a wooden bucket, and a rope. From behind a huge boulder, a few feet farther back, an old Indian woman wrapped in a black shawl walked slowly past. "Excuse me, where are the ruins?" I asked in broken Spanish. She did not speak or even glance my way. I turned my head to see if anyone else was nearby, and when I looked back she was gone. I had temporarily lost my bearings. After several hours of wandering, I reached the village sometime after sundown.

I never did find those ruins, but I had touched upon a reality that will endure long after those stones turn to dust.

As I walked among a group of villagers returning to their homes, I had no inkling that another fateful encounter was only a few hours away.

Some questions appeared later:

How can I continue if I live in this fog, in which seeing and doing, consciousness and will, remain artificially separated?

Can I "intend" facts, or are they attracted solely by my state of being?

NOTES

[1]P.D. Ouspensky, *In Search of the Miraculous* (San Diego: Harcourt), 1949, pp. 22-23.

Notes on Meetings with Remarkable Men

Prelude

Many years ago, Lord Pentland was speaking before a large group of us soliciting donations for a film. The film was *Meetings with Remarkable Men*. Following his short announcement, solicitation, and call for questions, there was only silence and more silence.

Finally, I spoke. "How can you make a film of MEETINGS when clearly many people who see it will not have read the First Series? Gurdjieff made it very clear that we are not to read MEETINGS before having read the First Series three times."

Now, the silence was even more profound. Someone had just openly challenged Lord Pentland; this did not happen often. Lord Pentland was not a big man. He was thin, rod straight, yet oddly as relaxed as an old suit of clothes. I think he was probably in his late sixties at the time, but most important was that, to all of us, he was Lord Pentland, the undisputed head of our Work in America.

I felt like a bit character suddenly thrust into the spotlight alongside the star: he could crush me for such impudence, and no doubt there were some who would relish that. Of course, he did something totally unexpected; he doubled up his fists and, in a roguish tone reminiscent of a barroom brawler, challenged me to step outside!

The room burst open with laughter, not a reserved tittering, mind you, but the deepest belly laughs ever to be heard in that Movements Hall. To make a long story short, he then asked me if I thought that the difficulties which people face today, life itself, had not prepared people in the world for seeing *Meetings with Remarkable Men*.

I said I did not know. Now many years later, I see a little better what he meant. To quote Bob Dylan, "There are many here among us who feel that life is but a joke; but you and I, we've been through that, and it is not our fate; so let us not talk falsely now, the hour is getting late."[1]

So, here are a few notes and reflections on that book and our current context. Gurdjieff gave us a taste of a new life, a good life that is still to come, if we can understand that there is a way forward.

Has something changed in the world? Has the extraordinary reign of violence that dominated the last century finally brought humans to the brink of reason? Tens of millions of people murdered and swept-up like so much garbage, neatly arranged under the label of War and Revolution.

Before the wars and revolution in Russia, Leo Tolstoy, suffering deep disillusionment with his life, the religion he tried to practice, his own work, began to ask the same questions. His answer, after much profound deliberation, was Yes. Yes, people were moving out of the delusions under which they had lived for so long. The shift to a more intelligent, fair system of government was on the brink of realization.

Looking back, it is easy to see how wrong he was, how his desire to see a change was stronger than his reason. I think we can all sympathize. Living through the sixties, we too, with much less reasoned thought, believed.

"To destroy mercilessly." It is an indictment; we will destroy human life and culture but not our illusions; that is how Gurdjieff begins speaking of the aim of the First Series, and we have certainly and perversely accomplished that. Like a giant stone wheel, once set in motion, it will not stop until it grinds and pulverizes millions of human bodies into the dust. Has this horror altered our inner passivity that allows us to be put into a killing trance again and again? This "periodic human psychosis," how can it be changed?

You see this is something we can answer only with our Work. All other answers are meaningless; until our own Work as a whole sees this, how are we to begin to influence the larger world? Are we each able to think and feel independently? If not, why not? What are we waiting for?

But these are all considerations belonging to the First Series, and now we want to enter the Second. And this is the problem: If we have not separated our self from this old way of thinking and feeling, perhaps not yet destroyed but at least are no longer enslaved to these old ways, then going on is prohibited, not by any external rule in the Work but solely due to our lack of understanding.

Can we say that it is given that life has forced us to see a little that we have lost our way; that we must, like the Prodigal Son, face our pigsty and think about returning home? Perhaps there has been such a small change of understanding. In any event, let us continue as if.

Notes on MEETINGS WITH REMARKABLE MEN

> "Egyptian priest first teacher of Moses—*Satisfaction-of-self from the resourceful attainment of one's set aim in the cognizance of a clear conscience.*"

MEETINGS demonstrates the interplay between wolf and sheep. It also reveals many other aspects of Gurdjieff's progress and the personal obstacles he encountered on his search. They may fit neatly on a Deus ex machina, but this cannot speak to flesh and bone weariness, suffering, and all the struggles we are heir to. These real life encounters are revealed in the characters portrayed one by one. Pogossian is the "bull" who labors consciously. Yelov is the sly one: boil seven Armenians; get one Aisor. Someday, Pogossian may become a sly man. The activation of the centers, the change from curiosity to fervent search is dramatically portrayed when Vitvitskaia nearly bites through her finger. Soloviev is the hopeless addict who finds objective hope and sincerity. They are all Gurdjieff; they could also be me and you.

Gurdjieff plays the ox and literally sweats to learn the secrets of plaster of paris; yet he is really the sly man. He too is a specialist in hypnosis like Dr. Ekim Bey and very interested in sorcery as well. He finds inner guidance through the healer Ez-Ezvournian on the use of Hanbledzoin and so on and so forth. It seems a rather candid and complete picture of Gurdjieff's inner life: rascal, seeker, and saint.

There are many cross or hidden connections that are only revealed through serious study of this book. Reading MEETINGS may seem rather simple after wading through the First Series; yet it is essentially a complete study of a seeker's inner life, as he searches for the Way.

For example: The work on the science of vibrations resonates between Vitvitskaia's interest in piano and Ekim Bey's interest in the telltale way the body vibrates with the direction of thought. Perhaps this work on the science of vibrations is predicated and grounded in the work of sensory presence practiced by Pogossian with the helpful guidance of the Dervish who has an understanding of the physical body and what not to do regarding breathing. This all of course must lead towards the healing of Vitvitskaia's inability to control her passions as indicated by her thyroid condition; to Yelov's eyes; to Skridlov's kidney ailment; all as a context and prelude to the teaching on Hanbledzoin and the Astral Body. The importance of the balance of these elements is taken up briefly elsewhere in this book.

Returning to the beginning, Gurdjieff's search is sparked on a note that is fundamental to modern civilization, a simple question, "What is true? What is written in books and taught by my teachers, or the facts I am always running up against?" These facts include miracles that cannot be explained by ordinary rational thought, which is too often our own science.

The First Series shatters the chains of our illusions. Now, in MEETINGS, Gurdjieff continues, saying we can begin to separate what is true from what is false—based on what? Based on facts we actually observe and constate from our own experience, knowledge we actually know, of course relative to our position between sleep and awakening. If we begin to know, to experience what is true, we are knocking on the door of this new life.

This new life begins when conditions are created whereby the wolf *(the fundamental and reflex functioning of the human organism—instinctive and moving)* does not swallow the sheep *(whole functioning of one's feeling)* in us.

To put this more simply, there is something aggressive, wolf-like, in us, something related to fundamental forces in the body, forces of the descending octave, lunar in nature and subservient to its needs, drives of hunger, survival, and sexuality, that naturally predominate the more passive feeling and self-awareness, unless the mind, in the role of deputy steward, enters the equation.

This inner relation has become less civil as our civilization, that is, the conditions in which we live, deteriorates. We live in a state far below that of animals. Separated by fear, we have lost our natural respect and common connection to Great Nature.

For this new relation, between wolf and sheep, to be possible, the mind *(that chief impeller to self-perfection)* must be developed. This relationship must be achieved in the state of remembering oneself *(that necessary factor in the process of self-perfecting)*. When some people in the Work denigrate the mind, they lose this main catalyzing factor.

While the ordinary thinking function has become passive and separated, (*from their individuality and thereby conscience has ceased to function in this thinking of theirs)*, active thinking is required *(in the conscious and conscientious fulfillment of my life obligations)*. It is the abstract question, the question that is not required by life, such as, "*What is the sense and aim of the being of beings*" that can lift us above ordinary thought, ordinary effort, and give us wings? What in this is difficult to grasp?

"Understanding is the essence obtained from information intentionally learned and from all kinds of experiences personally experienced. One must strive to understand; only this alone can lead to our Lord God" (MEETINGS).

There are those in the Gurdjieff Work who "believe" in the Work on sensation, believe that this aspect of Work alone leads by some magic to a three-centered existence. Who can think like this, when Gurdjieff is so clear that effort itself must be three-centered? Yes sensation, yes feeling, yes pondering; yes, yes, yes and more.

> So that we won't fall into this trap Gurdjieff simply paints us a picture (egoplastikoori). He tells us that *with his force of logical confrontation and intensity of feeling there simultaneously arose the "whole sensation of myself."*

It is a portion of what Gurdjieff defines as a "remarkable man"; that is, *"resourcefulness of his mind . . . and who knows how to be restrained in the manifestations which proceed from his nature, at the same time conducting himself justly and tolerantly towards the weaknesses of others."*

His father was alert in his mind and gifted with a phenomenal memory maintaining a *calm and detached inward state in all external manifestation throughout the misfortunes that befell him.* He never tried to make a profit from the misfortune of other human beings. Somehow this state seemed directly related to his meditating on the stars in the night sky.

We hear of a certain substance that can be acquired, a substance that can exist after death, something finer, a soul. This soul begins its development from the physical body and continues through the astral, mental, and finally the divine body of man.

Gurdjieff tells us that if we are to count on help from above, we need a soul. A soul is the vessel; if it is unfinished, old, or torn, it is a vessel in name only. It is then unable to incorporate higher forces. There is no sentimentality here; no wishful thinking will help; either we assist the arising and perfecting of our soul or we cannot expect help. We are simply unprepared.

Priests at one time were also physicians, treating both body and soul. As Gurdjieff makes very clear in his booklet, HERALD OF THE COMING GOOD, no change is possible unless certain fundamental conditions in the health of the body are addressed. This includes dealing with all kinds of addictions.

In MEETINGS it is prescribed that we must also find a companion who is of a corresponding type. Gurdjieff indicates that this is crucial to completing our individuality and supporting the growth of our own unique typical manifestations. In other words, we become less related to our essence if we are paired with the wrong type. Helping to make these determinations was also a function of the priest.

There is a fundamental principle of intentionality that runs like a red thread through this narrative. It is the "*Law conformable result of a man's unflinching perseverance in bringing all his manifestations into accordance with the principles he has consciously set himself in life for the attainment of a definite aim.*"

This means ideals and aim must be related. Where does Gurdjieff speak about these ideals? They are incorporated as the qualities of these remarkable men by the way they approach their life and search. When is it spoken about in our Work?

This question also touches on the Third Series, LIFE IS REAL, ONLY THEN, WHEN I AM.

NOTES

[1] From Bob Dylan, *All Along the Watchtower*, ©1968, 1996 by Dwarf Music.

The Place of Gurdjieff's Movements Within the Greater Work on Oneself

In response to a question reflected in the title, it may be useful to have some insight into a much publicized component of the Gurdjieff Work in order to bring Gurdjieff's Movements back into meaningful context within the greater psychological and cosmic scheme connected to the arising of an esoteric school.

Forms always stand below the level of substance from which forms are made; then, once forms are created, and by this I mean esoteric forms, it is necessary to fill them with Hanbledzoin, but if one does not understand this, the forms remain pathetically empty of life.

Thus, in trying to clarify hierarchy, to begin to give some context to those forms that are obligatory and then forms that are useful, one must start with authentic group work which can evolve into its fully psychological and cosmic functions. Higher and more subtle functions remain unknown and unfulfilled in groups outside the Gurdjieff lineage.

The Source of these esoteric forms is the result of a process unseen by those without discrimination through whom these vital forms designed for psychological evolution degenerate into adornment for the ego. Here is where the kernel is separated from the chaff.

These forms must elicit conscious activities connected with our three centers, our two natures—with self-observation, self-remembering and sensing, non-identification, external considering and so on. It is clear that the practical study and application of the ideas of the Work must take precedence over all forms of Work which could be viewed as their outgrowths or appendages.

A growing knowledge of the Law of Three and the Law of Octaves, then, as one of the Obligonian strivings, is of primary importance. It is rare to find someone who rightly values real ideas, ideas that come from on high. These laws are not mere words, but potent influences descending and branching lawfully from the Logos itself.

Those without experience of being touched by ideas of different levels take them as ordinary objects or associations and give them little value. Gurdjieff says that pondering of such ideas should occupy one third of our time. When we begin to value these ideas, it becomes relatively easy to see that all the powerful intelligent forms of our Work arose and must continue to arise directly from applying these very high, very refined ideas to our situation.

Gurdjieff found a number of effective means, interventions, and restorative measures in order to deal with the imbalanced and poverty stricken psychological state of humanity and in particular of those individuals who are seeking a Way. He realized the appalling lack of preparation in the seeker to enter a Way; this lack included a dearth of attention, and, in particular of free attention, which is one of several of the reasons that Movements are important for students.

Usually after a certain preparation students like myself were given the opportunity to study the Movements within the conditions of a more organic, sane, and comprehensive Work on oneself. This addition helps inoculate the forms from becoming infected by false personality and self-love. A very few made a specialized study of Movements and were, after many years, given the authority to teach Movements as a support; but the teaching of the Movements was never separated from the true Source.

The central and indispensable form of our Work is Group Work; it provides that unique set of conditions Gurdjieff would utilize to bring students face to face with themselves and others under the guidance of a teacher who had lived this Work. Gurdjieff intended that this teacher would be a man or woman who had applied Gurdjieff's ideas to him or herself and had digested the experiences over many years, learning the lessons necessary for transformation from man 1, 2 and 3, or mechanical man.

The sacred interaction of Ideas and Forms, can give rise to a Substance necessary to create a higher platform, a higher body, upon which ever new possibilities and responsibilities may evolve. So, to return to forms, forms that lead us towards consciousness and transformation, we must begin with the relationship between student and teacher.

From the birth of magnetic center a sensitivity develops that can recognize higher influences; it may find itself attracted thru B influences in theatre, art or music, true craftsmanship, dance or ideas, but primarily it is in search of another human being who incarnates, to some degree, that conscious state which the seeker is wishing to attain him or herself. The seeker is looking for palpable proof that conscious evolution is possible. It is why the center or leader is so central to the group.

In Gurdjieff's Work, leading towards the 4th Way, this fundamental teacher/student bond is modified by the obligatory introduction of Work within a psychological group, itself both penetrated and alive within a cosmic dimension. As it is said in the parable of the Centurion, each is under authority and gains authority, knowledge and power to heal as it serves this higher purpose; this is known as faith in the Gospels. With the help of certain teachers, I was able to study the creation and maintenance of Work conditions in all their complexity, difficulties and opportunities naturally occurring in a large Gurdjieff Foundation, and also to visit other centers within and also outside the Foundation.

Following close upon this relation to the teacher, one must come to a direct experiential study of the ideas as tasks and exercises as they are applied in life and in the forms of the Work—many of these come underneath the great formulation, Know Thyself. The major textual resources include: IN SEARCH OF THE MIRACULOUS and ALL AND EVERYTHING. Careful reading of these books leads to focused exchanges and recapitulations in a study group.

At some point one begins to experience Gurdjieff sittings with their special arrangements and themes acting as a potent medium; they may be silent or guided sittings which can bring a very high influence into one's body and its seven centers.

Then there is Work in the Arts and crafts—one can get a feel for this by reading in ALL AND EVERYTHING concerning the Adherents of Legominisms. The following are some of the forms that act as linking grounds for the development of different capacities generally or subjectively necessary in preparing one to enter the Fourth Way. Very often there are Movements, form and color—painting and related arts, theatre, writing, translation, music—instrumental and vocal, pottery, cooking—as in Gurdjieff's time the preparation of the first being food and the head of kitchen is given an important place. There may be all kinds of auxiliary activities like making meditation cushions, flower arrangement etc., and the preparations for each January 13th opens the door to a plethora of creative activities.

There are many situations designed for exploring the Work with others, the second line of Work, for a conscious socializing, for external consideration, and for self-study; in this second line there are many relatively invisible activities because they are simply taken as 'Teatime' and so on.

There is also physically demanding work—this should precede a student's introduction to the arts and crafts—including Movements. Note: This requires practical knowledge of seed preparation without which a right valuation for the form may be sacrificed. There can be construction and remodeling of buildings—various types of gardens, housework, and maintenance; in some cases farm animals have been raised. It does not help however to follow those who imitate the forms, to enter a pretend Work.

There are many forms of special Work and tasks. I remember well, for example, co-leading the children's daycare and also watching Dr. Langmuir lead the teenage work, both of which refrained entirely from any kind of indoctrination. It was a Work to support the right growth of essence and in that loving light all who guided it were fortunate. Different essences have different possibilities; for example, Gurdjieff speaks about those who come from a special caste of humanity capable of developing healing powers of Hanbledzoin—magnetism; which he says he acquired to such a degree, that no man, perhaps not even in any past epoch, had been able to acquire. This capacity is a defining characteristic of Gurdjieff himself.

There are a myriad of special group and independent studies—one such special private sub-group I led in the Foundation was on understanding the growth of higher being bodies; before and after leading this study group, I found it helpful to consult and confer with a number of people.

Speaking of this, Gurdjieff said that no productive Work (this of course includes Movements) can occur before certain abnormalities in individuals have been addressed. It is quite rare in the deep, hypnotic sleep in which we live, and with all the negativity we call our emotional life, that someone enters the Work without some serious defect which they are blind to; these include addictions, mental and psychic aberrations, excessive anxiety, tensions and fears, and various kinds of corporeal health problems. As it was said in the Bible, one cannot pour new wine in old wineskins—or patch a tear in old cloth—but this is what many without understanding try to do.

At the same time one can see that people have different gifts; it is certainly wonderful to see those very few with the gift and courage to become genuine Movements teachers: those hearty ones who have not taken the easy way despite strong individualism. They are the disciples of Gurdjieff who have subjected themselves to the liberating fire of his Work. In Movements, this was exemplified for many of us by Paul Reynard: a man who incorporated wisdom, power, and ability.

Different people have different functions, as I observed when I was young in the Work. At that time John Pentland directed the Work in America as a whole; Paul Reynard was the head of Movements, someone else the music, others in form and color and so on.

Movements and the full spectrum of Gurdjieffian forms represent powerful tools to awaken a sleeping humanity. Yet we have wandered so far from anything natural or sane; we live more and more an imitation life and are tempted to follow imitation teachings. We forget that a tool can be constructive or destructive; a psychological tool is most constructive within the natural matrix and essential place of its origin. That is why a sincere person, a person who wishes to teach within a specialty area that Gurdjieff himself created, must have sufficient integrity and common sense to accept that they must simultaneously be initiated into the whole authentic Work that Mr. Gurdjieff gave to us.

Remember, Ouspensky was also given the title of specialist by Gurdjieff, of course not in the area of Movements. It is the same with all who are leaders in the Gurdjieff Work; each will have one or more areas of specialization. If and when you enter the Work, you will also find that there is an objective work designed for all and later a subjective, personal work designed especially for you.

Remember one very important thing. All the living forms of the Work are created to serve the aim of our conscious evolution towards or within the Fourth Way. So use your head and think before letting the tail wag the dog.

Warm wishes to those who Work.

Will – The Way

Gurdjieff's Work is unfolding. As with the system of Ashiata Shiemash, it is renewing itself, for it is not a set system. It is the elaboration of a seed planted 100 years ago in Russia. It is a "work in progress," but there is no guarantee that it will continue in the same direction that Gurdjieff envisioned.

Many mistakes have been made; many important elements that should not have been forgotten have been forgotten. "Accustom yourself to forget nothing," Gurdjieff said. Even during discrete phases of this Hermetic process, the process of the whole must be understood. Certain ideas, methods and techniques are emphasized for a time, become central, and then pass into the subconscious; they are put temporarily to one side.

This phenomenon is true not only for individuals but also for the whole organism we call our Work. Those who do not understand process are unhappy with change; certain things are left out, for the moment, and certain seemingly new ideas come to the fore.

This process of change takes people by surprise; they have heard of shocks but are not prepared for them. Madame de Salzmann, Michel de Salzmann, Lord Pentland and others introduced such shocks to act as leaven, and inevitably there is resistance. This resistance, that part of it which is not built on fantasy, must continually be reincorporated to produce the results we need. This resistance, oftener than not, begins when we stop questioning ourselves, our opinions and attitudes, our personal prejudices and preferences. It is a sign of aging, not age, but aging or petrification.

Now we have continued, awkwardly, a bit rigidly, yes; but that was to be expected. Creating a line or square of will, which must now be decentralized, we must open up dramatically, organically, to a larger life force; we must breathe, bringing dynamism, balance and harmony to all the varied functions. This development is represented by the fifth step, and, as with every change in number, there arises a change in form; and this change must fit the corresponding discordance of our times.

It is here that external and internal branches develop, where the coming perfection or wholeness must be allowed to touch and reunite our efforts. Those who lock themselves away in a defensive posture cannot save themselves from discord; in fact they invite and perpetuate it.

Nor can we go on simply by mechanical momentum. As Lady Pentland once said to me, "Your Work in the morning does not pay for the afternoon." We are not prepared to meet the challenge of this fifth stopinder as we are; a new initiative is needed. When Madame de Salzmann developed four centers, the development was appropriate for the time to help us cross the mi-fa interval. Now that the Work has completed a circuit and returned to Russia, a fifth center must be included.

This Russian center is not just one more center; it is the completion of the foundation of our Work. In the 100-year centennial we celebrated the inclusion of all Eastern Europe into the Work—just as one must include all the five lower centers—bringing them together—to draw down and spiral upward to connect to higher centers.

This double appearance of the number five, is it just coincidence? Perhaps, but Gurdjieff's life, and one can say his influence, is atomized in all we do; such coincidences were frequent then and are now. Five is the number of Man; one cannot stop at four, which has concentration but no dynamism, i.e., will without faith. Russia represents this faith. "Begin in Russia, end in Russia," Gurdjieff said. To Quote from Churchill following the first victory for the allies in WW II, "This is not the end, not even the beginning of the end, but it is the end of the beginning."

At the same time, this new initiative must refocus: a group must form that renews the original search, to climb that mountain; nothing is over, and nothing is finished. A new Seekers of Truth must arise, a core group, that can serve as the active side of awareness, returning us to the original course Mr. Gurdjieff set for us. We must begin to regroup ourselves around a new initiative, which returns to us from the Source.

Handbook on Energy, Pathways, and the Higher Bodies in Man

A Primer on Inner Alchemy

Focusing on Direct Experience

Learning of the Subtle Channels

Eliminating Blockages and Toxins

Reconstitution the Sexual Energy (Si 12 or JingQi)

Circulation of Life Energy

Preparing the Ground for Transformation

Essentials of Human Energy Transformation

Introduction

This is a very condensed manual. Its objective is to describe a high relief map of the way energy may become transformed consciously, so that our higher bodies might fully arise, become coated, and perfected.

The text is conceived of as a support and reminder to those who have a firm foundation in the Way of conscious evolution. This manual should be used only by the serious, sincere student or researcher. No guarantees are given, and the reader should consult his/her physician regarding any pre-existing health conditions or concerns.

Gurdjieff realized a very comprehensive and detailed approach to complete human metamorphosis. However many important aspects were buried very deep. One of these is the precise knowledge of energy (chi or prana) pathways. Gurdjieff speaks about prana but strangely he does not indicate its pathways, which are very well known both in ancient India and in ancient China. This knowledge is absolutely essential to the harmonious development of the human being. A lack of knowledge of these pathways would be similar to a cardiac physician's not knowing the vascular system; it makes impossible the practical application of alchemical knowledge. "The great masters of all the traditions are called alchemists." (Gurdjieff)[1]

Exact mapping of energy pathways is found in another ancient Fourth Way school called the Tao. Gurdjieff points to these teachings in ALL AND EVERYTHING.[2] Choon-Kil-Tez and Choon-Tro-Pel, twin Chinese princes and direct descendants of the Society Akhaldan, rediscovered the Law of Ninefoldness, the seven tone scale, science of vibrations, including the law of combination of colors (later transmitted to the Persians), and the Law of Three.

Their invention connected to these laws, the Alla-Attapan, is something that can be created within us: opium (Si 12) (neurohormones); sound (Sol 12) ('mantra-tuva,' throat singing); light

(Mi 12). This information was transmitted through genuine initiates (see YELLOW EMPEROR'S BOOK OF INTERNAL MEDICINE).

It is quite clear from the strong endorsement of Gurdjieff related to these ancient Princes, and therefore to the teaching later known as Taoism, that Gurdjieff meant us to research thoroughly these teachings on energy pathways and transformation leading to the development of higher bodies, as well as the laws of vibration that were of paramount importance in this ancient Fourth Way School.

Gurdjieff speaks of his travels in many places around the world. In BEELZEBUB'S TALES he indicates that some of the descendants of Society Akhaldan moved to the Gobi area before it became desert. Then when the sands came they descended into what was to become ancient China via the Yellow River. But he does not mention that he himself traveled here; why is that?

He promised to speak about the needs and possibilities related to the arising, growth and perfecting of the higher being bodies. This can be found by studying the entire corpus of his teaching, for example the Food Diagram. Lord Pentland told us, his students, we needed *to practice the Food Diagram.* The fire within is the Active force; food, air and impressions are put on the altar and sacrificed in this fire, creating higher energies.

My hope is that the information here presented represents part of Gurdjieff's promise fulfilled. However, I am solely responsible for any distortion or anything lacking in this manual. The teachings presented herein are drawn through and irrevocably entwined within me from primarily two sources, which I have studied and utilized for over four decades: The Fourth Way teachings of G.I. Gurdjieff and Taoism.

A map is abstract, a symbolic representation of an area's geography, roads, mountains, and streams you may encounter when and if you really begin the journey. You can imagine this journey, read about it, and this can help you decide whether you want to proceed. You may gain some idea of the difficulties and what preparations are needed. Or, you may only dream you are going on this journey. This duality that exists between one's essence wish and the intentionally actualized projections to materialize thought and one's opposing fantasies must be clearly seen.

In this New Age many equate their astral traveling dreams and fantasies with actually being a real traveler on the Way. Only experience in life can teach; neither the fantasy nor even the intelligent use of imagination is sufficient to make real changes. Edgar Cayce said, "Mind is the builder." This overseer must consciously engage, breathe in, and assimilate the real experiential material of our lives to raise and complete the energetic structure of higher bodies.

This process requires a special courage to wish to see and accept our ordinary and quite mechanical self. Persevering in the spiritual deserts, thirsting for consciousness that seems just out of reach, we begin to realize the importance of embodying this crossing of spiritual with the mechanical forces.

It has taken me over 40 years to put together the clues and find the sources in Taoist alchemy and other places Gurdjieff indicated, to complete the transmission regarding development of higher bodies and their subtle pathways, and their connections to higher centers. In addition to these main themes there is a myriad of other lesser facts that must be integrated in order to have a real result.

Often we find ourselves fighting nature, as a man afraid of drowning flails in deep waters. It is imperative that he relaxes, that he discovers the waters of life will support him if he can give up his fear. He must discover this bit of knowledge before he drowns himself. He may begin to see that he is fighting nature, but nature is not only immeasurably more powerful than he is, it is the very substance of his life. Instead of fighting nature, he needs to begin to live within Great Nature more consciously.

Since the terrain is ever changing it does no good to cling to a fixed method. A good strategy has tactical flexibility, allowing one to maintain the aim while meeting the actual conditions of life in this moment.

Or, perhaps for you, it would be better to forget all this and immerse yourself fully in the mesmeric dance of life. Transformation is necessary only if you cannot live without it.

I wish to thank Masters Kai Ying Tung, Marshall Ho'o, Ju kim Shek and Master Shenfushi for their kindness and patience; Lord John Pentland who was head of the Gurdjieff Foundation until his death in 1984. John Pentland was the first man I met who could demonstrate that higher being bodies exist and could be intentionally utilized.

My thanks also go to my friends in the Gurdjieff Work, especially Jack Haer, PhD, Dr. John Lester, and Norma Flynn for their kind suggestions; to Manfred Blum for a helpful exchange; and to Michel de Salzmann who responded to questions concerning my own Work on higher bodies in a way I never expected, re-vivifying that initiation begun over 36 years ago by Lord Pentland. (RIP All.)

Table of Contents

Preparation:

Seed of Mortality / Immortality

I. Orientation

Seeing, I pretend

Poised without stress, seek out a-live experience. (See chapter on "Three Fundamental Barriers.")

> 1. Relax the forehead, and let the head be drawn up as if pulled gently by an unseen hand from the top. Allow the attention to accumulate within the hollow between and behind the eyes; this is the Cave of Original Spirit and the third ventricle of the brain. It is where are situated the higher centers (higher intellectual, higher emotional) vibrating within the pituitary and pineal glands, swimming in the ultrafiltrate cerebral spinal fluid.
>
> 2. Let the tongue relax so that it curls slightly upward and touches the roof of the mouth. This acts as a bridge, connecting the House of Spirit, or heart and all its creative and vital force, with the conscious force descending into our bodies from above. The necessary development through both energetic and psychological exercises of those specific energies required to create higher bodies is found in the twin efforts of Conscious Labor and Intentional Suffering. The first gathers and elaborates what is to be sacrificed; the second provides the fire to sublimate and fix these energies (see "Enneagram on Baking Bread").

Fire is a Solar symbol for that which accelerates activity and vibrational rate–what makes conscious evolution possible at each level and destroys that which is impermanent. Slowing down, in terms of inner vibration means to fall into sleep and finally death as one descends the Ray of Creation towards the Moon.

Mme. de Salzmann speaks of the alignment of the spine as vital to the descent of higher energies into the body. However, there is another alignment which links the front of the body, as spoken about above, that is equally vital. A portion of this can be seen in Gurdjieff's exercise of dividing attention between the foot, solar plexus, and the head brain.

> 3. Saliva naturally accumulates and fills the mouth. The head being suspended lightly from above, the neck gracefully lengthens like a swan as it swallows. The intent is for the energy component of the saliva to descend below the navel. This substance regenerates the feminine aspect of the sexual energy. (See note in Appendix)

II. Reconstitute and Circulate the Vital Sexual Energy

Giving and taking in each gesture, in each moment.

The most potent and precious substance elaborated by eating food and drink is sexual energy. It is also the subject of the greatest misuse and fantasy. (This is related to Kundalini which is described in the chapter "Seeker and Addiction.") Sexual energy (Abrusdonis and Helkdonis) is the key base transformative agent that can eventually free us from the mortal coils of our physical body. But here great care is needed to avoid other more invidious chains. One needs a precise road map, correct mapping and picturing (Egoplastikoori), not vague allusions, but a clear guide to development of higher bodies. Intent must arise from both clarity of mind and sincerity of purpose, not from a desire to manipulate.

In the Gurdjieff Work as in the true Tao, the aim is to be conscious. The full realization of this aim is subject to the development of higher bodies. This development must integrate heat from both psychological friction and the 'fire' from the intentional stimulation of vibration in our energetic natures. The higher bodies or vessels (in the Bible referred to as "wineskins") are able to assimilate and incorporate progressively finer energies. Then these finer substances elaborate even more subtle ones which can be projected and distributed for the benefit of the practitioner and for other beings.

The first process, steps 1-3 and many inner health related activities, simply strive to replenish the life force stored as sexual energy. The second part, steps 4-10, makes sacred by removing impurities, which have become mixed with the sexual energy (jing qi; Si 12) so that it is unusable for evolving a higher body or reinvigorating one's life force and basic health.

> 4. When sexual energy (Abrusdonis and Helkdonis) and fluids are fully animate, breathe in slowly, and by simple projection, (picturing) of wish-intent, raise energy from root sexual organs through the base of the spine to mid-back (see diagram: a-b-c-d). Pause here, breathing to cleanse. Breathing outward, allow the finer elements in the air and sex energy to gently settle and mingle. This is connected to the first conscious shock and the development of Prana, H 48-24-12. Simultaneously, the cruder part descends (d-c-b-a) to its origin at the root of the genitals.

Sexual energy is unstable before it is transmuted. This energy is rarely assimilated *upwards*: if, in addition, the body does not have sufficient natural sexual or creative outlet, the resultant force will involve back down the system, poisoning the body (involution of Si 12-decay).

Highly volatile, the sexual energy becomes depleted or aberrated, passing unseen into tensions, anxieties, and worry. Particular concern is the combustion of this energy through intense emotional displays. Explosive emotional episodes are often a symptom of sexual disease. Even modern psychology recognizes sexual suppression as the basis for neurosis. The underlying physical-energetic cause for this universal dis-ease is concurrently a direct obstruction in the evolutionary path. If one wishes to generate the vital transformative heat, Zernofookalnian-friction is needed. It is vital to restrain emotional energies through conscious suffering, facing difficult situations and restrictions in fulfillment of desires and primitive drives.

5. Raise this energy again, breathing in (a-b-c-d); pause to allow separation of heavier cruder elements to descend and lighter finer elements to ascend naturally; then inspire to assist this lighter energy to ascend further (e-f to g), to draw this subtler energy towards the top of the head.

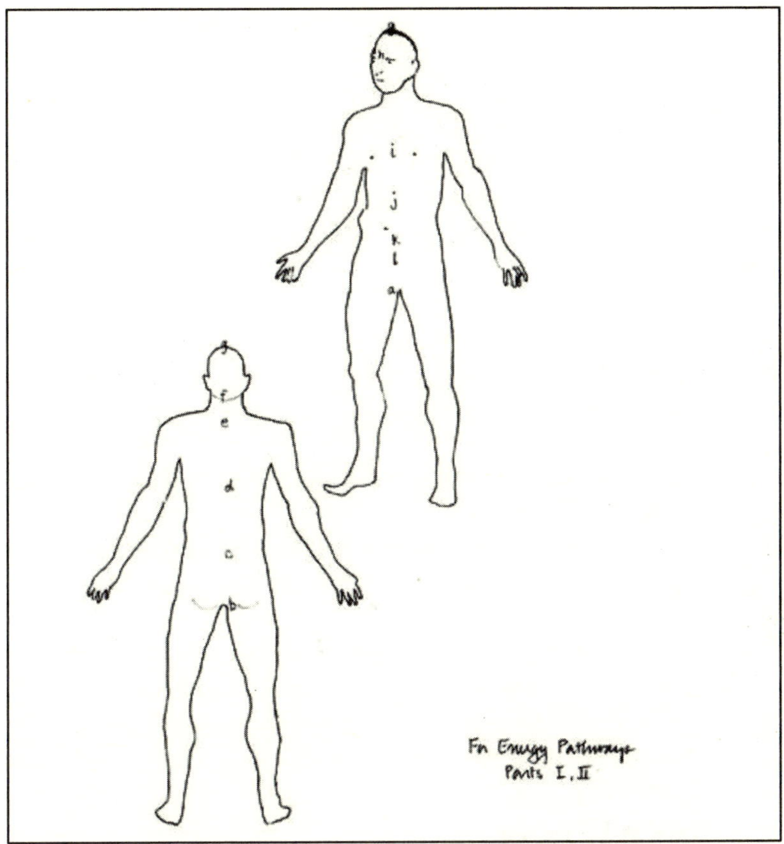

From the top of the head, this energy descends in front (g-h-i-j). Pause in the Solar Plexus for a breath, allowing this energy to be further purified. This is the lower half of emotional center that spreads its influence through the sympathetic system.

> The lesser, cruder energies going to nourish the sympathetic nervous system are calming the adrenal forces (H 24 and H 12) and turning them towards a spiritual warfare and away from ordinary fear and violence.
>
> The finer energy descends (k-l) to be savored and warmed in this container by the heating element below it.

The heating of this purified sexual energy, vivified by Prana (Breath of Life--solar energized gasses/air), will transform this still passive energy into a more active evolving energy.

This graduated induction and refinement of energy reduces the chance that aberrated energies associated with Kundalini will attempt to "take heaven by storm." The true alchemical liberation of the elixir of life is the antithesis of this. "In patience, possess ye your souls." (Luke 21:19)

> 6. The heat in the lower abdomen should now stir the positive sexual energy (in l, see above). The breath-energy absorbed in the lungs and liver and passing down through the Solar Plexus into the lower abdomen can now blend with this evolving sexual energy. The Seer directs his/her attention like an electro-magnetic pulse from the third eye that destroys all debris in the space ahead, clearing the Way for the process to continue unadulterated (See page 58, ALL AND EVERYTHING, Saint Venoma).

This energy is polarized toward evolving, but at this stage it may easily flip back like a magnetic switch towards physical procreation or pleasure. If, after several months of practicing the first five steps, the heat or energy is lacking, and the genitals do not become stimulated, then the overall health of the organism needs to be improved first before going on. (See Appendix to Reconstitute and Circulate the Vital Sexual Energy.)

7. The breath also acts like a finely focused bellows, fanning the fire under the alchemical vessel holding this precious substance. The heat causes the substance to evaporate, naturally rising with the inspiration up the spinal energy channel (as in step 5) and then descending through the Tongue Bridge to the origin where it is again heated and sublimated (a-b-c-d-e-f-g-h-i-j-k-l). This completes an outer circuit of this Temple of Man or Cosmic Wheel of Life.

Self-awareness and attention, that is, attending in each moment to what is actually happening, acts like a special spiritual magnet, attracting the finer, more vivifying breath that drives the distillation process at this level. To be asleep now is to invite trouble; for, as it is said, "A cleaned yet unoccupied house invites not only one's old devil back, but he will take with him seven other spirits more wicked than himself. And the final condition of that man is worse than the first." (Matthew 12:45) Although couched in religious terms, this is a piece of sound psychology, and the warning should be heeded in *all* future efforts.

After more time of clarifying and consciously perfecting these efforts, come to a tranquil, alert, and more awakened state. Go through with utmost care all seven previous steps awaiting the positive and now sublimated sexual force.

9. With the attention fully grounded in the sensation of the whole body, bring one-half attention to the inward space between the eyes (Third Eye-higher emotional center).

10. Allow the spiritual energy from above to descend (Law of Falling) into the lower abdomen and transmute this offering. Breathe-in to absorb this transmuted sexual energy into the spinal gathering place, directly behind the navel (c). As you breathe out cruder particles, the residue of energy combustion, are exhaled while the finer

> particles are sealed in the spinal marrow ("passive-moving center").

A note: When breath is utilized to draw energy from one location to another, it is helpful to imagine that one is breathing *from* the place one wishes to move the energy *to*. For example: when we wish to move energy from the lower abdomen to the gathering and storage area in the spine, it is as if I am breathing-in from the spine at point "c," drawing with the breath the energy from point "1."

III. Clear the Primary Energy Flow Circuits

(Gurdjieff's teachings on central axis [as "pipeline," "duct" or "axis of attention"] through which Ray of Creation passes and breaks into side octaves or branches)

Purpose: Removal of blockages which promote disease and impede normal energy transmutation and the transformation of our lives. (See also the chapter on "Seeker and Addiction.")

This is a physical process to assist the recognition and finally the removal of the psychophysical burdens generated by fear and from ignorance. These burdens include grasping of transient power and materiality, both ordinary and spiritual, judgment of others, opinions, and all manner of masks that one wears unconsciously.

Note: The exact placement of the centers and flow lines needs to be sensed and felt rather than imposed from an idea in the head. These centers and flow lines, like mountains, valleys, and rivers of the Earth, exist independent of our knowledge. Become gradually acquainted with them with the help of the "maps," but do not take the map for the reality. For example, organs in the human body are not necessarily in the exact place where you would find them pictured in an anatomy book.

> 1. Without pausing at any point, begin as in the previous exercise to breathe-in and raise energy in spine to the top of the head; then down the front of the body to the root of the genitalia and back to the spine. Repeat exercise until the flow is

natural and needs little assistance. Continue to watch, reducing entry and mixing of egoistic influence that would further taint the life force.

Looking down: Picture for the moment this basic life essence as a horse that has lived with harsh treatment. The task, of gaining its confidence to accept the reins as a positive connection rather than as slavery, requires great care and patient perseverance. It is connected to Prana, conscious breathing (Mi 48 – Fa 24 – Sol 12).

2. So that higher intelligence controls the reins guiding the process of transformation, the next step is to reverse the natural flow of step 1. The higher intelligent energy comes down from above and enters the fontanels or Hundred Meeting Places (the soft spot on the top of a baby's head), where the whole body is re-presented as in a spiritual assembly awaiting the descent of God.

Looking up: Opening to the descent of this energy is a test of all one is and will be. This is why an active critical faculty, which can discriminate between truth and illusion, must guide but not interfere. Patience and openness are the operative qualities required here.

3. Once received, remain open (breathe in) and accept this descending force, sensing and allowing it (breathe out) to flow unimpeded from the top of the head down the spine and up the front of the body in opposition to the former direction (g-f-e-d-c-b-a-l-k-j-i-h). Remember to retain the tip of the tongue lightly at the roof of the mouth. Maintain this flow until it has become natural.

The process described above will have a gradual calming effect on those chaotic forces arising from below. You have to see the growth of these two diametrically opposed forces that have been seeded and grow in us: the natural life force and the egoistic aberrations. The seeing will allow for a gradual separation of the good from the bad, useful from the useless. (The actual removal of the "weeds" as it is identified in the Parable of the Sower must wait until later.)

The destructive elements suspended and circulating with the life energy are being generated like poisonous fruit from a false egoistic tree. Increasing circulation and natural elimination can lessen the effects. The continuation of this exercise does just that.

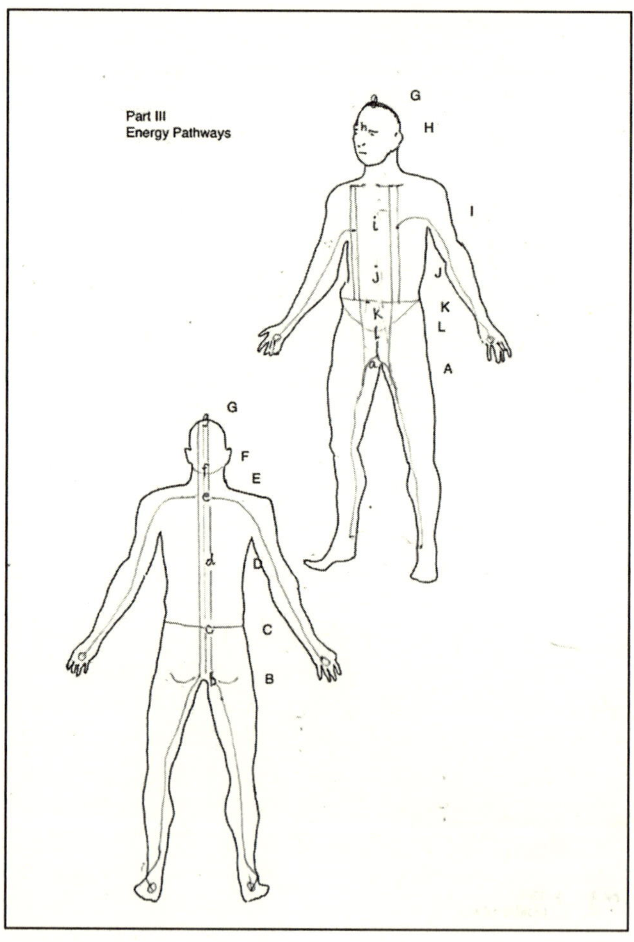

4. Allow the flow to go around 49 times; on the 50th circulation, let the energy descend (breathe-out) only to the Gate of Life or spinal gathering point (c) in the spine directly behind the navel. Here (breathe-in) the flow splits in two, moving around the back like a belt attached at the navel. Imagine it is a very wide belt, like a sash that also touches the point between the navel and pelvis (l). Let the energy gather in the front and be nurtured by the breath (7 breaths).

5. On the last out-breath, the energy divides in two, rising up from below the navel in two parallel lines about ½-inch from the centerline. It rises to just below the clavicle bone (near the windpipe).

6. From here, breathe-out, allowing the energy to move outward along the clavicle (two inches from the centerline) and down two parallel lines through the nipples to the lower abdomen and back to the sexual center (l).[3]

This breaks up obstructions at this level and acts to separate the coarse from the fine, helping to sublimate the vital energy through rapid succussion. Allow at least 7 revolutions here to loosen build-up.

7. After the last rising breath, as you begin to breathe out, the life energy follows the clavicle and descends to the nipples. From here energy flows further outward to the axilla (under the arms). Then, it flows down the inside center of the arms to the wrists, warming the center of the palms. Breathe-in from the palms gathering energy here.

8. Breathe-out as the energy rises along the outside of the hands, up the center back of the arms

to just outside the spine at C7-T1 (at the level of the shoulders). Breathe-in to gather energy at this yang accumulation point.

9. Breathe-out to lower energy down two parallel lines about ½ inch from the spine. This continues down the back and outward descending in the middle of the buttocks and legs to calves and then to outside the ankles and center of feet. Breathe-in through ankles and feet to gather energy.

10. Breathe-out so the energy ascends along the inner ankles up the inner legs and thighs crossing under the genitals and reuniting at the point below the abdomen (l).

11. Breathing here from this point, allow energy to gather, but do not concentrate; relax to avoid creating premature crystallization, blockage, and aberration.

12. Then, breathe-in from the lower back (c) and let this energy rest and be stored there without covetousness.

This point (c) is called the Gate of Life. It is where prenatal vitality is stored. Directly opposite this point is the navel, where post-natal vitality is concentrated. In ancient teachings it is said that we are given 8x8 or 64 units of this vitality at birth, and as we express our energies in life (Bobbin kandelnosts), we lose this vitality. This process of returning post-natal vitality to restore prenatal vitality, is designed to reverse this loss. Much of the abnormal loss of vitality is through negative emotional dispersal of sex energy.

These two points are connected by a channel called "the belt channel" or "girdle." This is the same concept as in the Bible where it is said "Gird up thy loins." Thus there is a kind of energy field that can pull up the sexual forces and returns them to the Gate of Life as a restorative. This is a method by which some ancient people were able to prolong their life. Remember the very long lives of Father Sez and Father Ahl.

This practice should be done daily; once the channels clear, the process can go on either without "resting" at any point or optionally with longer rests. Concurrently with this activity, practice inner listening which will help you follow the rhythmic spacing and other subjective changes needed to harmonize your particular system. There should be no invention, only that deep inquiry into the needs of the system to be sustained and evolve.

To increase the power of the process, breathe into the lower abdomen now, as if starting a fire from kindling. Parallel to this, it is necessary to restrain emotions through non-desire and non-identification and to bring the resultant heat (wish) into the lower abdomen rather than let it be dispersed (see Food Diagram Si 12, Sol 12, Mi 12).[4] Desires and instinctive drives are Lunar in nature; non-desire turns this force around so it begins to arise from Earth towards Sun, which is connected to Essence-Wish. Transformative Heat is derived through a crossing of psychological and energetic processes. As the lower abdomen warms, energy begins to expand and ascend naturally and circulate as described. Do not stimulate, and leave this sexual energy here unless the purpose is to act as an aphrodisiac, which is not the subject of this essay.

Sweating may occur spontaneously during these exercises. This sweating helps clear the skin, blood, and energy circuits. Sweating by artificial means, sweat bath, sauna, are also valuable but should be carefully monitored to prevent excess loss of moisture or salts and exposure to cold.

Intermediate Stage

IV. Elemental Balance

The spectrum of life energy is diffracted into seven subsets of vibration. Each of these is housed in particular organs of the body with corresponding functions. Here we will touch upon only one level, the emotional function expressed as joy, sympathy, pathos, fear, courage/anger, integration, higher perception.

Exercise:

Sense each organ as given, and feel the related emotion; then feel the two opposites together.

Joy is a natural expression of the heart. In the opposite direction come the winds of pathos. Literally, the inspiration of the breath of life infuses our lungs and we experience/feel the almost metallic taste of sorrow as we measure how far we are from the animating spirit. Simply follow the breath as it enters the lungs and combines with the venous blood in its endless circuit from right to left.

Like a massive tree erupting from a small seed, courage, power, and growth are the functions of the liver. When frustration becomes anger (hot-bloodedness), this condition disturbs the connection between the body and the emotions. (See ALL AND EVERYTHING, Piandjoehary, p. 761.) True fear is instinctive, potentially clairvoyant perception vital to preserving us from danger. It is a function of the kidney/adrenal organ. Life and death can be viewed together.

In the center is sympathy, the feeling that can relate and ground opposing pulls of the other four. It is found within the digestive system, spleen, and pancreas. It is designed for nurturing and centering but may degenerate into an enfeebling saccharine sweetness. Be still and allow all the pulls of the body to settle in the navel area, which will act like an anchor, drawing these five elemental forces (joy, sympathy, pathos, fear, courage/anger) towards the center.

Finally, the whole of the circulatory and sexual system is taken as one organ-like function, the big heart. This is a feeling that encompasses all the emotions. Com-passion is an inner acceptance that absorbs all the diverse passions and returns them to their essential source, the Self. Only an all-pervading and encompassing feeling of remembering the whole of me, of *all* my parts can bring this to fruition.

Meditation on these emotional qualities, their physical substrates in the organs and tissues, and the linking ground of the blood, requires time. (Intentional suffering is letting go of emoting or emotional identification ["self-expression"] to acquire feeling toward Self Remembering.)

Completion

V. Carnal or Earthly Energy Body

In returning to stillness

Return and complete the process up to #11.

If you have continued to practice daily, you may be experiencing increased emotional balance, at least during meditation. We will proceed to gather this outer alchemical agent, clarified and reconstituted sexual energy. It exists at the highest point of the physical process and therefore closest to the "foot" of the Astral Body.

Sexual energy exists as doorway between the outer world and the inner world. As an agent of nature it generally is pulled towards an outward expression, either the desire to have sexual relations, to have children, to be creative in life, arts, technology, etc. In the worst case, it backs-up into the emotions or body, creating disease.

We are at the crossing here where the outer agent is precariously sought by both inner and outer forces. Like a "thief in the night," a representative from either side may appear and take you with them.

The outer agent which you have gathered in the spine (c) has slowly matured like aged wine. This process may take a lot of time and repeated turning of the wheel of transformation. An important condition necessary for maturation is to separate from the desires of the body; the outer pull must be reduced. We must assist the arising of non-desire over desire, especially when we meditate.

> Still the body; eliminate tension to aid the natural flow of energy and breath. The heart is unstirred and the mind unfettered by thoughts.
>
> 13. Breathe-in and direct the energy concentrated in the lower abdomen (l) up the abdomen in the channel ½ inch from the centerline and down through the nipples to complete the circle. Continue until this succussing becomes automatic. This process activates the maturing agent, like

shaking a "test-tube" as in homeopathy to separate and remove course from fine.

14. When this agent begins to vibrate in the lower abdomen, stop the succussion and breathe-in with the intent to isolate this energy so that the heat and pressure begin to increase. Breathe slowly directing it as you would to bring embers to full fire.

If genitals become aroused, lead the energy back up into the area of the navel. If this fails, *press at the root of the genitals to prevent emission*; repeat above until calm. It is similar to gaining control in ordinary sexual intercourse. *Note: any forceful suppression here can cause real damage. Be careful; I have seen some testicular damage from this wrongly practiced by following Mantak Chia. It would be better to stop and gain control through gentle restraint in sexual relations.*

15. With mind-body and awareness together as one, roll eyes seven times counter-clockwise. This will assist the arising of the alchemical agent up the spine. Then roll eyes seven times clockwise, causing a counter swirling effect that will mix the energies in the brain, increasing absorption and blending. This also helps harmonize the left and right brain and helps dissolve third barrier. (See chapter on "Three Fundamental Barriers.")

16. The outer agent is transmuted into positive vitality. There is a sensation of peace; anxiety and worry disappear. Let any residual energy flow down the front to its reservoir below the abdomen.

This practice nourishes the brain, connecting the outer agent with the nervous system, spinal center, and the body as a whole. It re-establishes the natural energy patterns and the Natural Energy Body. It can reduce susceptibility to diseases of all kinds and may lengthen life.

Note: It is vital to bring together attention, awareness, and sensation to assure a harmonious result. If it is not yet possible, it is better to stop and work on each of these steps until it is possible. These are obligatory and fundamental in the Gurdjieff Work as it was in the distant past when there still existed schools of true Taoism. Also be sure that the energy spreads to every corner, every cell of the body to the utmost of your ability (both a Tao Principle and Lord Pentland's admonition). Any blocks should be overcome before proceeding which may require specialized intervention or exercises such as massage, chiropractic work, acupuncture, yoga, or tai chi chuan.

VI. Solar Plexus Energy Body (Astral Body)

Assist the recollection of the whole over the expression of any part.

One attempt at collecting the positive vitality will not be enough. The gradual process of restoring the whole system may take a fairly long time. When positive vitality and the systems, from which vitality arise, are fully restored, it is like having a lamp full of oil; at any moment, a flame may cause incandescence.

> 17. It is said that a bright light will emerge from the Mysterious Gate. When the outer positive (positive because of ascending, i.e. evolving) yin (Si 12 and Sol 12) vitality (oil) meets the inner yang agent (flame), their union is verified by the manifestation of the golden light.

Perhaps you will have brief glimpses of this light as you work towards filling the lamp with the oil of positive vitality. It is better not to strain or attempt to hold onto the experience. Later, when conditions have become right, the Golden Light of Original Awareness will appear strong without flickering.

> 18. When the golden light[5] is stable, focus your eyes inwardly without tension toward the third eye. When this light resides peacefully within the

> brain, a finer energy residue begins to filter and settle. Breathe out and down, directing into the solar plexus. This brings together the outer golden light with the inner active solar plexus substance. The union of Solar forces within and without the body causes the solar plexus to emanate the Light of Reality.

This Light can grow only in utter stillness and silence. The evolution and involution of all my Being, outer and inner, begins to balance; something closer to the **I (Master)** may occasionally appear between these two primordial currents, a taste of freedom to come. But, as we have all heard, this **I** can become permanent only with the death of that which we have come to know as "I," even that which has led us to this point, awakening, death, and only then, true rebirth. This brings us to another major aspect in our study of what may make possible our evolution. It can be found in Mr. Gurdjieff's and Ouspensky's books.

Note: At any point in this long process one may lose one's place, become imbalanced, or forget oneself and why effort is needed. Do not become disheartened; you are in good company. As Rumi said, "This is not a caravan of despair" so shake the dust from your feet and "Come, come again." "Even if you have broken your vow a thousand times, come again."

> 19. Finally, the escalating involution and evolution of forces moving down and up through the body may be felt more intensely than previously experienced. Gather this true light, drawing it down and direct it to enter an inner cell within the lower abdomen (l) to produce the immortal seed.

> 20. Settle down; roll eyes counter-clockwise to raise energy through center of body, eyes closed. Focus conscious attention (light) from above head through the third eye (g to h) to the seed (l). When saliva fills mouth, swallow to bring this nectar down to nourish immortal embryo (l).

The process of nourishing the immortal embryonic body with light and nectar requires time, in optimum conditions perhaps months.

VII. Pineal Energy Body[6]

If thine eye be single,
the whole body will be full of light
(Kesdjan body of the soul).

21. Restoring the immortal breath begins by drawing light from Heaven above the head through third eye (g to h) towards back of head (medulla oblongata—above brain stem, see the chapter "Three Fundamental Barriers, Third Barrier) and down to the soles of the feet.

22. From the soles of the feet breathe in to lift Earth energy and true vitality up the spine and into the back of the brain and forward to the third eye (h). The third eye is where this intermingling may create a clear fluid that can, if sufficiently saturated with sacred prana, crystallize into a "pearl." When the pearl between eyes (h) begins to radiate a golden- moonlight, it indicates maturity of the immortal embryo.

Pulse and breath may come nearly to a complete stop when true immortal breathing begins. The event stabilizes the Spirit/Conscious Light. Do not attempt to induce these changes artificially; they must be a result of the process; again, this process is not an imposition from the head or ego.

23. Roll eyes clockwise to blend white conscious light with the golden light within the pearl. This creates an electric-blue current, which opens the Third Eye.

The whole body is surrounded and pulses like the Aurora Borealis potentially generating an all-pervading light. If light is weak and flickers, or if hallucinations or psychic attacks occur, stop and start over. Maintain your body heat and avoid loss of semen.

> 24. Re-enfold energy into growing immortal embryo of Pineal Energy Body (I). Utilize conscious intent to close all orifices in body to energy loss. When vibrations become intense, assist this energy to rise up spine (pinch base of spine if needed). Roll eyes clockwise to raise, then counter-clockwise to internalize into the brain. Then close eyes to gaze at Light and Rainbow Body.

Gradually Pineal Energy Body will mature with all its powerful psychic functions. Avoid clinging to likes and dislikes, attitudes and judgments.

The pineal gland and the pituitary gland (the father) are connected to the central nervous system through the superior cervical ganglion. The pineal gland inner octave is the higher emotional center (the Power). The pituitary gland inner octave is the higher (Logos, thought, or intelligence) intellectual center (the Glory). In addition, these are the brains of the body Kesdjan and Higher Body Kesdjan of the Soul.

When you breathe, the air, Hydrogen 192, enters through the nose and mouth. One part entering the lungs goes into the blood stream; the other part enters the nose, rising as ions through the olfactory epithelium into the brain (see Society of Legonimism on the sense of smell[7]), its outer function, and the appearance of an inner function). When the ions in the air are consciously absorbed as impressions, and the air octave progresses, simultaneously, Hydrogen 48, H 24, H 12, H 6, H3, then we are intentionally activating the connection to these higher centers directly. Try to understand this as a breakthrough in the psychology of man's possible evolution.

VIII. Diamond Energy Body

(Second or Higher Kesdjan Body of Soul-the Immortal Soul)

When two or three are gathered together in my name,
There I am.

These three bodies, the Natural, Solar, and Pineal may merge in the right conditions, forming a fourth body. It is said that active forces of each may blend, creating a perfect triad, crystallizing into an immortal Diamond Body.

Emergence

IX. Freedom of Being and Action

To swear with the saints, there shall be time no longer.

25. Focus through the all-pervading light as it blazes. Use Conscious intent to launch one's inner body out through the top of the head. Gaze down, then up to make leap.

Emerge in calm inner and outer conditions; avoid electro-magnetic disturbances. Returning immediately, gradually extend time, distance, and experimentation. If a Golden Wheel of Light appears, suck it back into the head and body.

Cleansing and serenity of Spirit result from the grosser elements being purged from the Soul. Then there is the gradual sublimation towards a totality of Self-awareness, the finer gradations of Divine Reason marking the final perfection, the crown or horns of the eternal Diamond Body.

NOTES

[1] Solange Claustres, *Becoming Conscious with G.I. Gurdjieff* (Utrecht, The Netherlands: Eureka Editions, 2005), 137.

[2] G. Gurdjieff, *All and Everything, First Series: Beelzebub's Tales to His Grandson* (Aurora, Oregon: Two Rivers Press, 1993), 341 ff.

[3] This direction is resonant with the directives given on p. 179 of "Meeting Thirty-Three, Monday 9 December 1946, *Transcripts of Gurdjieff's Meetings 1941-1946* (London: Book Studio, 2009).

[4] P.D. Ouspensky, *In Search of the Miraculous* (San Diego: Harcourt, 1949), 190.

[5] Michel de Salzmann is remembered as saying, "It takes gold to make gold." In Fran Shaw, *Notes on the Next Attention* (New York, Indications Press, 2011).

[6] The pineal gland is made up embryologically of eye tissue; it is literally a third eye. One scientist called it a multi-oscillating coupling system, linking our body's biorhythms with the cosmic biorhythms.

[7] The sense of smell is connected with our deepest emotional memories, who we are, even who our ancestors are. It is a deepening form of Self-Remembering.

Appendices

Appendix to Preface

Ancient Egypt's School of Materializing thought; China-Tao—Law of Nine foldness, development of immortal embryo; India—how to deconstruct kundabuffer, coating with Prana and perfecting Higher Body.

Note. Is Beelzebub the great god Pan? Did Beelzebub help Jesus? When asked, Jesus does not answer. He instead, answers with a question of his own. Is there a parallel to Solomon the Great, who uses Daimons to build the Temple? And by trickery and sacrifice of ego and the ring of power, he tricks Asmodeus so that he, Solomon, can fulfill his aim to get Wisdom and complete the Temple of Man.

Note. On Egoplastikooris: "I decided to do this in order that many diversely essence "Egoplastikooris' for your future logical confrontation should be crystallized in corresponding localizations in your common presence, and also in order that from active mentation the proper elaboration in you of the sacred substances of Abrustdonis and Helkdonis for the purpose of coating and perfecting both of your higher being-parts should proceed more intensively."[1] From hydrogen 48 to hydrogen 12, and in addition the energies are purified by the "heat" of Zernofookalnian-friction (the source of heat and suffering) to create the alchemical agent needed for transformation.[2]

Appendix to Orientation

Note: after Orientation #3: See ALL AND EVERYTHING[3] p. 1911, "to have faith, whether consciously or even unconsciously, is for every being very necessary and desirable and it is desirable because owing to faith alone does there appear in a being, the intensity of being self-consciousness necessary for every being, and also the valuation of personal being as of a particle of everything existing in the universe."

Appendix to Reconsititute and Circulate the Vital Sexual Energy

To understand the transformation of emotionalism to wish, and through the fire we need—read System of Archangel Hariton in ALL AND EVERYTHING, pp. 70-2.

NOTES

[1] G. Gurdjieff, *All and Everything, First Series: Beelzebub's Tales to His Grandson* (New York: E.B. Dutton, 1950), 1165-1166.

[2] Ibid., 1168-1169.

[3] Ibid., 1911.

[4] Ibid., 70-72.

The Sacrifice

What is the nature of the sacrifice? The sky above; the earth below, a table is set; the sacrifice is laid upon it. There is an invocation of powers. A fire is lit; the sacrifice is consumed.

Symbolic.

In one's self, food enters the mouth, and the fire within the body cooks the food, consumes it. We are constantly in the process of sacrificing. Air, sound, sights enter us like food, and the active energy, the fire within, consumes it.

I have a desire for something; I have a fear that I can lose something; the sacrifice is to the moon.

The active energies in the body are like heat; they accelerate the speed. They act upon the passive energies entering the body. Without this heat there is an inability to transform and step up the ladder of evolution, the Food Diagram. Conserving heat is imperative to maintaining life. However, it must be balanced with water, or life is destroyed.

For example, food enters the mouth and stomach and is acted upon by enzymes and hydrochloric acid, and the food is transformed into a new substance ready for the next step in the long chain of steps called digestion and assimilation. The active energy is always heat, compared to the passive energy which is always water, and the resultant is always steam.

So heat is simply an accelerated state when it combines with a decelerated state (a lower consciousness). Then a result is obtained that lies between higher and lower. This is a sacrifice: the lower being made sacred, in comparison to its former state.

By the sacrifice of the higher entering into the lower, combining with it, the higher thus loses its former state. On each level fire and water retain their relative differences of energy but change the level of their activity. When we reach the end of what nature has provided for us, at Si 12 in the Food Octave, Mi 48 in the Air Octave, and due to the aberration of human life, at Do 48 in the

Octave of Impressions, then, by necessity, we need a new kind of fire to enter the process.

It requires a special conscious and intentional effort to bring this fire to the table of sacrifice. To consume this sacrifice, whether it be Si 12, Mi 48, or Do 48, since the greatest treasures lie in the highest hydrogens, Gurdieff has us focus on impressions and within them are inner octaves, within which are also higher hydrogens.* However, if we focus on Mi 48 of the Air Octave, we can combine directly the further transformation of air or Prana, and at the same time put fire to the impression of air. This is a secret at the center of ancient alchemy that has now been revealed. The nexus between the psychological and energetic is reintegrated. The psychological friction of conscious labor and intentional suffering is the transformation of Prana, by the heat of this sacrificial fire, achieved energetically. Another way of picturing this idea as a process is to say: The psychological friction of conscious labor and intentional suffering, created energetically through the heat of this sacrificial fire, becomes the transformation of Prana.

NOTES

Read p.297 P.D. Ouspensky, In Search of the Miraculous on objective music.

"Higher centers are the palpable manifestation of inner octaves, materialized in us but cut off from our lives and experience due to a lack of "binding energies" such as carbon 12 needed to transmute Do 48 of impressions into Re 24, and Mi 12 . . ." - AF

*The finer energies that exist within the more material energies. The octaves are there but they are discontinuous. There is a kind of break that has to happen in order for the inner octaves to become a part of our lives. The promise is there in potential, but it has not been fulfilled or realized.

Webinar with Alan Francis and Arkady Rovner on "Sacrifice"

Moscow, Russia, Spring 2015

Part I

AF: In order to begin, we have to start somewhere. So, because this night is dedicated to the idea of renewal, to sacrifice and renewal, let's begin by sacrificing our associations, anything that holds us to this wheel of life. So, let's take one minute of real silence. That means not just inner silence, not just stopping one's movements in the body and the emotions and the mind, but also anchoring oneself to this deep silence that is within us. So, let's just make a test for one minute of silence.

O.K. Welcome tonight. Thank you for coming out on this very beautiful spring day in Moscow. I'd like to welcome you here, and my guest, Arkady Rovner, who has graciously consented to come and speak with you and me. Many of you know Arkady from his numerous writings and philosophy, in Gurdjieff and other subjects, and his seminars and talks throughout, so I welcome you Arkady, thank you for coming. (From Arkady: Thank you.) And thank you (to audience) for coming. At the beginning, we made a tiny payment, of silence, but that payment is just for the moment. If you wish something more than just words, then you have to pay with your presence and your attention. When you were a child, you spoke like a child; now that you are an adult, you have to speak and act like an adult.

We are going to have a great deal of time to take your questions and also your statements, anything you want to say after Arkady and I speak. And we both hope that you will speak your minds, speak your hearts, and ask those questions that are your most important concerns for your inner life. While I was walking here from Kurskaya, I was looking at the faces of the people I passed and, of course, trying to be aware of my own face, and I saw many, many people unconsciously suffering. You see fear, anxiety, you see jealousy, you see all kinds of expressions on their faces, which they are not conscious of.

There are two ideas about sacrifice. One is unconscious sacrifice; we are sacrificing our lives to these negative emotions. So it's your choice whether you want to sacrifice unconsciously or intentionally, consciously. Your emotions are the most powerful thing in you. They control you. You have to make a determination if you want to lose this life force through your emotional excesses or you want to begin to restrain these emotional outbursts and these anxieties appearing on your faces. And, in doing so, begin to take back your life so that when you say, "My life," it actually begins to be, your life.

Let's try an exercise together because words are not so important. The words that I say, or somebody else says, or you read, they are gone in a very short time. But if you have an experience connected to words, to ideas, then they remain inside you. It reminds me of the old Chinese saying, if you give a man a fish, he eats for a day; if you teach him how to fish, he eats for a lifetime.

So, just very simply, I want to remind you of. . . (AF goes to white board with marker and begins with two circles, one far below the top one). Let us take the idea of the witness. Right now it's possible that you could be witnessing your life. So I am witnessing myself standing here talking to you. Are you witnessing yourself, now? Can you see yourself? O.K. So, this relationship between the witness (AF writes the word "witness" above the top circle), which is the conduit of consciousness, and the doors of perception (AF writes "doors" next to the bottom circle). So, as I am writing, this connection, at the lowest part of my nervous system, connecting with what Mr. Gurdjieff calls "Hydrogen 48," this is telling me I am holding this marker, sending information (AF moves other hand down arm holding marker). So, how could we be connected between the doors of perception or eyes, or ears, or nose, or hands . . . and the witness? In order to be connected, we have to have this tremendously open space (AF draws egg-shaped oval around line connecting witness to doors). If this space is full of associations, whether of the mind, the emotions, or the body, then this conduit, this linkage between the highest in us, connected with the Ray of Creation, all the way down to the lowest part of us, is blocked.

So, immediately, the idea of sacrifice has a specific and special meaning that is here, a sacrificing of all the mechanical associations that I have thus far lived for. If this, for example, were the sun, and this were the moon, then we have to make this connection between the sun and the moon. And, in order to do that, we are going to have to sacrifice our attachment to these associations. Some of you can now see your thought process, at least superficially. So now, as a thought enters your mind about what's being said, or about some association having nothing to do with our being here—you can observe it. And, the power of seeing, if you really do see, is so strong that it is an absolute for your associations; in other words, it can dissolve the associations. But, if you are attached to your associations, if you like them so much, then they will be stronger than your wish to see. So, you have to make a choice. Do I wish to be conscious, or do I wish to stay a machine? Do I wish to start next year, or now?

Now, what stands in between this very high level in us (and this is not the highest level because we are not starting with the absolute)? It's like they say, you have to talk about the name of God; well, you can't name God. It's like the name Tao; if you name the Tao, it's not the Tao. So, the way that exists between the highest in us and the lowest in us must be cleared. And this is like an electrical shock that has to come from this high level. (The Sun is electrical.) It has to come from this high level and pierce all these mechanical levels. What's in between? (AF draws 6 horizontal lines inside the egg shape). It's the whole Ray of Creation; it's the whole world in us. And so, once we begin to clear this pathway, we then have to replace this old mechanical process with a new conscious process. And one of the first things we have to do is look at the pictures we have of ourselves, which Gurdjieff calls "Egoplastikoori." (Big word, one of his strange words that he has in ALL AND EVERYTHING). What picture do you have of yourself that prevents this conscious force from entering you?

Let's take an extreme example of this kind of false picture. What happens when a young girl pictures herself as very heavy? But actually she is losing weight, and soon she is going to die because she is becoming skinnier and skinnier, but her picture of herself is still that she's fat. This is a false Egoplastikoori or a false picture of herself which has become so extreme that a young woman may starve herself to death because of it.

The fact is that the picture you have of yourself is slowly killing you. That false picture makes impossible, what is called in the Bible, "the straightening of the way." This straightening of the way was the task of John the Baptist, who many people think was one of the heads of the White Brotherhood. This straightening of the way, comes before the entering of the highest principles inside of you. First you have to clear the way; then you can have these higher forces enter you.

At each level, one could say there is a kind of table or place for sacrifice. So, at the lowest level here where Mr. Gurdjieff says that some obstruction was created, that this obstruction, which he called Kundabuffer, and which is represented by three spirals, three and a half circles actually, takes the highest energy the body produces, which he calls Si 12, creative or sexual energy, and the Taoists call Jing Qi. (I don't know if there is a special name in Yoga for it; is there a special name? Audience: kundalini? Yes, that's the problem.) What happens is that the sexual energy is taken by these three and a half winding circles, which is actually a snake wrapped around the sexual energy, and then all kinds of imaginings, all kinds of false beliefs, begin to connect with the sexual energy. So, to sacrifice these false pictures about sexual energy and to determine exactly what it is and what it's purpose is, acts as this first level of sacrifice. And, as we know, this energy and the ideas concerning it, like you in the churches and various places in religion, are totally disconnected with the organic function of sexual energy. So, in the Taoist tradition, this energy has to be brought to this particular place and a fire lit under it so that it is sublimated. The Taoist's is more of an energetic approach, while Gurdjieff's approach is more psychological, at least externally. And what I've been doing for a number of years is working gradually to relate these two: the energetic and psychological.

Part II

AF: Sacrifice, in the original etymology literally means "to make sacred." You want to turn this negative vitality from moving only outward, to also moving inward and upward. (See "Handbook on Energy, Pathways and the Higher Being Bodies in Man.") Then it becomes positive vitality. Only when it becomes positive vitality can it begin the work of transforming this energy into higher and higher vitalities until finally you create an immortal body. And this is also called "the Soul." If you wish to gain a soul, if you wish to live more fully, not as an automaton, then, you have to be willing to sacrifice your energies which naturally are either blocked into imagination or are being used only externally. These are the energies that one ordinarily uses to gratify desires. You must begin to cordon off desire with non-desire.

Up here, on this level, the solar plexus, you have emotions connected more with the body and the sympathetic nervous system. These energies, right now, are being used up constantly with anxiety and with fear. And they are being extracted from you, pulled out of you. So outside situations that cause you to be afraid, to be anxious, pull your life energy from you. And then once you begin to witness this, and you notice it is true, you are responsible, now, for your energy. So, what do you choose? Do you choose to sacrifice some of this external energy, externally restrain some of this energy so that the emotional energy of the body, which would then be connected with Sol 12, which is fairly high level, but it could also be 24; it could also be Fa24. Then you begin to Remember Yourself. And when you begin to remember yourself, you begin to feel why you are here.

Why were you born? For nothing? Just to live an existence of pure crap? To be manure? In fact, it sounds better, *merde*. Very nice word. Or, do you want to begin to come back up, from the lowest level of mechanicality, come back up the Ray of Creation and begin to exist at a higher level of being? If you do, you have to collect yourself. We are so used to throwing ourselves out there, what we call "self-expression," that we never really come inside ourselves, never experience who we are. So, in a way you see that sacrifice, or making sacred, is a kind of suffering. We have to let go of old things; we have to let go of the person that we think that we are, that we have pictured ourselves to be. Then we can begin to become ourselves. Essence has gone all the way down to the bottom, and we can begin to bring it back up. Our true self comes from the stars. It is not a metaphor; not an abstraction. It is reality. If we wish to come back to our true self, we have to follow this return path up the Ray of Creation. And so, at every level, we must give something up, to get something new.

Question from Russian interpreter: What would be the next step after the solar system?

AF: The heart. Connected with higher emotional center. And then, depending upon which arrangement you have, you can go up to the mind. And the mind goes to a very high level. We are going to have time for questions, right after Arkady finishes his talk.

Arkady Rovner is presented (applause).

Part III
Questions and Answers

Question: Mostly inaudible, but pertaining to the need for Work ideas.

AF: You know, one needs to be very practical. When you build a house, you have to use—especially if you are building it alone—you have to use pieces of wood to stabilize the walls as they are going up. If you are building a larger building, you need a scaffolding (it's a structure that people climb on) and much of these teachings are that kind of a thing; they are kind of an artifice. And once you build the building, you take down the artifice, but without the artifice, how can you build the building? Behind the artifice, there is a reality that we are looking for. All the theory that we use is a kind of artifice. It's not the reality. But it leads you towards that reality. Once you open the door and you step through, you don't need it. Right now it is possible to step through the doorway of perception. It's possible. But it's only possible if you made this effort for the last two hours; if you didn't pay, you won't receive.

Question: Pertaining to development of higher energies and bodies. AR answers. All in Russian. Translation inaudible.

Another question: (inaudible translation).

AF: Gurdjieff describes in metaphor the way in which the spaceships are propelled. He describes a number of steps that are necessary in order to develop higher energies and higher bodies. So for example we talked about this way of movement (gestures to the chart on easel), it is a way of movement that he calls the Law of Falling. And that it is possible, if you get out of the way, to allow the energies to fall down to the area below the abdomen. This is the beginning point for transforming Si 12 and Sol 12 (inaudible).

Question: Pertaining to Michel de Salzmann, but inaudible.

AF: There is not much I can say except that he was very gracious towards me when I spoke to him about my long study in this area of higher bodies and he knew about that study. Then I had had a separate secret group within the Foundation for several years. We spoke about that group, and he simply told me that I would be attracting many people to the work and starting centers, and he gave his blessings to it. But I never met somebody who had that level of not only development, but of harmonious development. He was really the result of Gurdjieff and Mme. de Salzmann.

Question: Concerning the Soul.

AF: So that's your question: if my soul can become immortal, has it always been immortal? Well, if we take an ordinary example of a young child, because our energy system is sort of like an embryonic soul, these energy lines exist in us, but they are very weak. So it is up to us whether we are going to mature those energies, grow those energies, until they become stabilized and crystallized, or whether we're going to let that embryonic body, or the embryonic soul, simply disintegrate. But everybody here has this energy; something of this energy exists right now in this room; it emanates from each person; some is shrinking because we are a little tired. But there is an exacting method by which you can grow, stabilize, crystallize this energy. That's your choice, whether that is something you wish to do. Gurdjieff said for a man without a soul, or for a man with a soul, all is roses. But for a man with a soul in the making, it's thorns. It's like a caterpillar that looks at a butterfly. It must go into only very specialized conditions in its cocoon. Can you imagine? It's like its body is dissolved in a sense . . . almost . . . to metamorphose this new life. That's why few people choose to go through this complete metamorphosis. And very few people today understand completely that process, even in the highest levels of the Gurdjieff Work today.

Questioner: Thank you. AF: Nods.

Question: I want to ask you about the Gurdjieff world. So, I will try to crystallize, in essence. Beside there are many groups, there are also point of view that after Gurdjieff, there was nothing left of essence in the teaching. But when you reply to someone of how to make a soul, your sort of propose a recipe book, a little bit, how to do it. Will you say that this view, that Gurdjieff is dead and so his Fourth Way teaching is dead, is true? Or, after Gurdjieff, is it possible to make a next version more relevant or more alive?

AF: Will you translate that briefly (into Russian) for the others?

Questioner: I am done.

AF: My point of view is that there is no one like Gurdjieff in the last thousand years. That is my personal opinion. He left some extraordinary human beings that had developed higher bodies of which I have absolutely no doubt. So, we are talking, at minimum, man number 5, maybe higher. This includes Madame de Salzmann, Michel de Salzmann, Lord Pentland, and others. What happens after a great teaching is a gradually descending octave of people, disciples, but there are the possibilities of people continuing to rise up to a higher level, and there are a few who have. Not only is there a series of steps in the octave (gestures to easel), but within each note there are higher octaves, inner octaves, and this is something we didn't speak about tonight. We have alluded to it; I think Arkady alluded to it. But this is a part of what is called "the sly man's way." Or "taking heaven by storm." (Arkady adds a comment in Russian at this point.) What will happen, I don't think anybody can predict. But right now there still is real Work, and there are now still real disciples of Gurdjieff.

AF: Last question, if it's a good question.

Question: In Russian (translation inaudible). AR answers in Russian (inaudible translation).

AF: So, it remains a question. What is necessary; what is important, for you? Arkady and I are here just to open the question. I hope it was an interesting evening for you. I thank Arkady and all the people who made this happen with video, and with the setting up, my translators, thank you all for your help. If you are interested in talking to Arkady, I think it probably will be easy to find him.

AR: I have a website, ArkadyRovner.Ru.

AF: Our website is under construction. But you are welcome to talk to Kate or Lena or me, Grisha, about our group. When you walk through the door, see if you can remember yourself. This whole night has been a kind of measure of yourself, of your interest in consciousness of higher things, and so you can take a measure of yourself. Not the picture you had before you came in, but the picture you have now, and that will be a sacrifice to help you renew yourself. So thank you for coming.

Applause.

And Hassein Wept . . .

As the stories of his grandfather take root, little Hassein begins to think and ponder actively. In time, his view of the world changes; he looks at the world with growing wonder, intelligence, and candor. But alongside the awesome beauty and majesty of God's creation stands the almost unbelievable stupidity, callousness, and the utter madness of man: his total disregard for these gifts. Hassein hears of the superhuman efforts, made by more conscious beings, efforts to change humanity, and he hears that man's feet remain covered with dust. This tragic play begins to act upon little Hassein: first, on his reason, and then on his feelings, which begin to cognize something disturbing for himself personally.

As this personal, inner realization automatically begins to surface from his subconscious, Hassein weeps. Like you and me, he is being prepared for his future role in life. For this evolution, the subconscious and the conscious aspects of his being would need to become intentionally harmonized. As yet, the nature of his new role and destiny remains invisible and unknown to him.

What is it that his grandfather wants him to see, beyond the natural struggle for Self's evolution towards consciousness? This evolution seems to be coming to an end here, on our Earth . . . unless a strong, conscious, and sustained shock can be absorbed and digested.

Hassein asks if so much had been given to him, so much prepared for his welfare by beings whom he did not even know, what was his responsibility?

Do I ask myself, "Am I but an unprofitable servant?" "Have I not hidden my talent out of laziness or for fear of finding myself at risk, even in trouble and grave difficulty?"

Some of Gurdjieff's most trenchant examples for us to consider are the Society Akhaldan, The Initiate System of Ashiata Shiemash, and the Adherents of Legomonism. Each of these had a tremendous impact, both in terms of direct "C" influences, culminating in initiation and "B" influences. The latter, hidden in many diverse disguises, have acted in the past as a leaven in the cultural dough.

How far have we explored the importance of "B" influences? Do they appear in only certain rarefied realms, or are they descending into objective scientific study, applications, and inventions in many diverse areas of art, rituals, and ceremonies to encourage ordinary people to take part and be enriched?

There were those farsighted people like Pythagoras or the Medici family whose activities spread into ordinary life. There are the Five Excellences and many illuminating concepts from Chinese culture which spread to the Japanese: Tea Ceremony, Ikebana, Haiku, Chinese Feng-Shui Gardens, or as common place a ritual as attentive precision in food preparation, Noh Theatre, Zen Meditation, and later Aikido. These are many forms connected with a search for a new valuation, patience, sensitivity, and consciousness leading towards a right development of humanity.

What forms might arise from the Gurdjieff Work? Do we not have an obligation to produce them? What type of forms penetrate most deeply and last longest? Certain very high level examples exist in art, of course: The Last Supper, the Sphinx. . .

But what binds almost unseen and most closely in ordinary people? It is certain repeatable ritual practices like Tai Chi Chuan, Yoga, Tea Ceremony, and "games"—chess from the Persian Magi, and from the Taoist, the I Ching and Go, the Tarot, and so on.

Are there potential new forms that may be created still? Should we help to perpetuate some of those existing forms that have survived from past cultures? This collecting, maintaining, and teaching of ancient forms that have relevancy today—is this not a good Work? Could this be the next step after we begin to come to terms with what Michel de Salzmann brought, and Madame de Salzmann? Again, I am not speaking of a mixing of teachings but rather a valuation.

All of these efforts to create and disseminate forms that lead towards truth seem very fragile when set against the truly stupendous dark tide of wars, ignorance, and sleep within us and in the world.

And Beelzebub himself: what were his tasks? We read that they were focused on stopping animal sacrifice, a common religious practice that was disturbing the equilibrium between nature, the Earth, and its relation to the Solar System. To accomplish this task, he needed to change the center of gravity of activity in several very large societies on Earth. How he accomplished this with two very different strategies is very interesting and very much related to our own struggle; but it is not within the scope of this essay.

The fact that Beelzebub was given this assignment and carried it out tells us that the scale of Work of higher beings with more developed being reason must be resonant with their level. A being must continually look toward his personal development first; that is the rock upon which all else depends. Yet when being matures, one's influence and responsibilities should also expand to include a broader set of relationships to include other powers and principalities commensurate with that stage of growth. One feels that as a metaphor this turning of our inner state away from destroying our own animal being also requires some very deep wisdom, and, as was said, two very different strategies.

Then, one naturally asks oneself, if the Work represents some evolving organism, what new duties lie on its horizon? When people in the Work begin to be concerned with humanity's continued downward spiral: the social and psychological degeneration, the environment—our environment, our Earth, genetic engineering, and so forth—what should the response of the Work as an organization be? Should the Work ignore these concerns?—or should it not begin to ask itself, as little Hassein did, "what is my duty here?"

Unfortunately, this brings a dubious rational to some who see this question in terms of black and white; many who seek to influence things on a larger scale lose contact with their inner work. And the truth is, very few people can honestly relate their inner Work to the World around them. There is a rather mysterious disconnect which reveals a lack of maturity of being from both sides of this dispute. And if there is no leadership in this vital interface, how then will the Work continue its own evolution from Sol?

In this isolated state, nothing really is accomplished. Those people who take refuge in the inner world from the duality of being and from others in the outer world, remain alienated. This phenomenon appears as alienation between people and positions in the Work, but in fact, it begins as an inner alienation. It is both unfortunate and ironic that this is a twisted projection of what Gurdjieff calls Zoostat, a wall between the subconscious and conscious parts of our psyche. And this wall, projected into the social structure of the work, becomes a source of continued misunderstanding.

Will we in Mr. Gurdjieff's Work overcome these splintering tendencies for a more intense living? Those who accept the necessity of attending to their inner work and simultaneously do not shirk the necessary next step of bringing this work into the world, into life, whether in small ways or on bigger scales, are the faithful ones, secreting God stuff, the substance of things hoped for.

The third world comes to those who psychologically leave father and mother. It calls one away from the brow of the hill and the opening door illuminated by bright warm lights which were the home of inner preparation, so cherished when we were a child of the Work. There was a preparation that was quite long but absolutely necessary; many times one felt the desire to quit. It is only those who do not quit, who come to the path of freedom and finally immerse themselves in the great stream of the Fourth Way.

But before this immersion, one comes to a lonely windy trail, then, a rocky and unknown descent to face. Who will go down, against logic, into that dark valley which each Pilgrim must traverse, barefoot and alone? There is a guardian of the Way who stays near; when Michael questions you, how will you answer him? Arrogance becomes like smoke, and choice is upon you: to go on that less trodden path or to return to familiar surroundings.

At this juncture, the path forward will not lead you upwards in the direction and in the states you have come to expect and desire. Rather, it will lead you downwards, putting you at risk and causing you to shed such comforts as soft clothes and shoes, powers and gifts already acquired by your conscious labors; for this is a trial by fire. Only those who have acquired something real, something tangible, will find the truth needed to continue and to fuse the Good within yourself into an immortal soul.

Through a Glass Darkly

A Short Monograph on the Teaching Style of Lord John Pentland and Some Cogent Comments Regarding the Future

Lord Pentland commenting on his time with Gurdjieff,
Half of the time, I was planning my escape.

There was a teacher whose word and gesture could act on one as a hieroglyph: Like the image of a foot poised to take a step. Pregnant with implications, pods of words could suddenly open, bursting forth with seed, leaving an indelible, concrete sense of spacious action, of setting forth towards an unknown star, which the Egyptians knew as a doorway. One of his closest disciples assured me privately that LP was Atlantean and Egyptian, working through higher mental center, and in this context we were related.

Listening to Lord Pentland was like turning a corner and finding oneself in a Socratic dialogue. Thought dutifully begins with Yes, yes I see; then, Wait just a minute, where the hell is this going? Wait, wait, a hopeful clue, a picture flashes upon the screen; then again it seems I am in a complete muddle. Then, possibly an inquisitive look from him, have you seen a little? Can you go further?

One could feel something hidden: a golden thread running through our exchanges, but lacking certain keenness, rarely could one follow it. Sometimes the attempt to attune was so intense one's ears began to come to a point. Only those who have tried know this is not a metaphor.

On occasion he would be looking straight at you and then very s-l-o-w-l-y turn his head to the side, often when you were still talking to him. The effect of this gesture was disconcerting, provoking a new inner question. For some it brought out internal considering and anxiety, wondering if one had said something stupid; various I's, that would not have normally, surfaced there and then.

Was the atmosphere rarefied? Yes, at times, but it was also simple and practical: awareness practiced as everyday duties, conscious chores, so to say; not running around seeking out something exotic, something outside of ordinary life to titillate one's sense of specialness.

Look, look over here! See what I am doing now. I have just received this special initiation from Lama or Sheik someone or other, and now I am bringing this to you. It is much like a cat carrying a dead mouse into the house.

There are vast treasures to be uncovered in the Gurdjieff Work; unfortunately there are few who have the fortitude to dig down to where Gurdjieff buried them. So it is with all the sacred teachings of St. Lama, Buddha, Lao Tzu, Zoroaster, and Jesus Christ.

We search on the surface of things (Do-Re-Mi—stopping often at the first interval, the first difficulty). When it becomes difficult, when we could discover something important, we jump to a different Guru where it seems for a while we have things easier. Many jump back and forth until all their possibilities have been fully exhausted. This subjective type of "zig-zag idiot" wastes everyone's time.

Coming to the core of our search, our own question: what is it we want, seeking what is alive in the moment—these were the things that brought out a special attentiveness from Lord Pentland. When this happened (I can say only for myself) the materiality of the room altered; shapes and faces shifted then. Well, others, mystics, have described such things better than I.

In the book, EXCHANGES WITHIN, a compilation of exchanges with his groups in Los Angeles and San Francisco, something of Lord Pentland's unique method of transmitting knowledge can be found. Although this is a faithful rendition, (I remember how carefully they were recorded), yet the whole picture cannot be transmitted, even as an accurate picture, without a feeling for his non-verbal style.

Now, we have all heard teachers bemoan the traps, obstruction, and tricks that formatory thought, the monkey mind, plays on the unwary student. There was something very different in Lord Pentland's approach. For example, it became clear that once we began to Work, it was no longer our right to spend too much time, that is too much of our attention, worrying about our behaviors: mental masturbation, emotionalism, bad habits; as it has been said, "Resist not evil." It may be only a coincidence, but I have found that those who most condemn the lower mind as the mind, for its obvious shortcomings, who therefore turn their Work away from the mind, tend to react habitually with a black or white dualism when they are confronted with something new or a shock to their own sensibilities.

What if they had begun to Work with their mind as Gurdjieff recommended and Lord Pentland so amply demonstrated; would they then be less subject themselves to that same monkey mind, the very same monkey mind that they abhor but unconsciously embrace?

By his example, Lord Pentland drew us towards a new level of thought. This new level of thought is not a rejection of thought, but an evolution, moving upward in the octave. This in turn opened in many directions; as Ouspensky recommended, we began to think in different categories. To do this we needed at least a change of state, if not being, and this was catalyzed by his presence.

Anecdotes and Such

Once when I was outside in the patio of a Workhouse, Lord Pentland came briskly out of the house, down the stone steps, and as he did, he spoke, "Energy is flowing off of me and no one is making use of it." He did not make statements like this very often. He wasn't boasting; he was simply stating a fact, asking each of us, why are you here?

At another time Lord Pentland was talking about how he had done something for someone, helped them out in various ways, and a person who hadn't remembered hearing him boast, asked in private, was that conscious acting? Lord Pentland replied, "No, in the Work we call that ego."

Sometimes after he spoke I hardly remembered anything he had said. At other times I would catch a thought deeply hidden and entwined within a long sentence. It would open like a flower in the mind; then the weakness of the embrace of my attention became more apparent as it was pulled apart: listen to what is next, or assimilate this denser thought, now?

A Little Background on Lord Pentland

Legend has it that the Knights Templar set off from Scotland to America before Columbus. When Mr. Gurdjieff placed John Pentland as head of the Gurdjieff Foundation in America, he gave us a true Knight and a conscious symbolist.

In the last 10-20 years a great deal has been published that links the St. Clair or modernized Sinclair Clan with the Knights Templar. Most recently a book and movie, THE DA VINCI CODE by Dan Brown has made their historic legacy and in particular the chapel on the Pentland estates rather famous.

With the recognition that Rosalyn Chapel and the St Clair estates constituted perhaps the last stronghold of the Knights Templar in Europe, there is a natural arousal of curiosity. Having studied with Manly Hall, who wrote the book on these groups, I was also curious. We, who find this sort of thing of interest, are also tempted to link the St. Clair line, later aka Pentland, with these ancient Knights.

Lord John Pentland, whose ancestors occupied the highest levels of society and politics in Scotland including prime minister, whose father was governor-general of Madras India, seemed destined for a life of power and influence. It is difficult to imagine all he had to lose by leaving Scotland and leaving his estates, breaking a thousand year tradition, and for what exactly?

Why then did he choose to give-up his birthright to champion the esoteric teachings of GI Gurdjieff? And why did Gurdjieff choose this relatively young man, a man who had only been with him for about a year (he worked with Ouspensky for ten years), to lead his Work in America?

This was a question, no doubt, many of the followers of Orage, Ouspensky, and others asked and argued over vehemently.

Speculation

It is an intriguing fact that none of the seeming countless investigators into these mysteries and conspiracies have ever unearthed or spoken about the strange connection between Gurdjieff and the St. Clair Legacy. Could it be that the esoteric Christianity that Gurdjieff was attempting to reintroduce into the modern world was not completely dead in Europe?

Gurdjieff investigated every type of occult, philosophical, and secret organization and said he found none that could be useful to his Work. Did he instead find a living remnant of the most powerful and secretive Knights Templar, the last initiate of the Knights Templar?

When Lord Pentland spoke to me about the two knights, one dressed in white and the other in black; of their meeting upon the field of battle, the one fighting for the good and the other evil, and asked me if that is the way I saw things, could he have been alluding to the Templars, who dressed in white with a red cross? Perhaps we will never know.

Yet there is a mystery here, and someone, someday will resolve it. Who was Lord Pentland? What if any was his link to the Templars, those mysterious guardians of esoteric Christianity? I am speaking of substantial historic evidence, some of which is readily available; not the speculation, right or wrong, that fuels THE DA VINCI CODE.

Whatever his true identity, it was well hidden in and from The Foundation. And certainly all this would not have been common knowledge among those vying for position in the Foundation. So there was a great dissension among those who thought of themselves as purer Gurdjieffians, and not just in New York.

At the Two Rivers Farm in Oregon, a separate fiefdom of Mrs. Annie Lou Staveley, Lord Pentland became persona-non-grata.

One could only imagine how the Farm could have benefited by working with Lord Pentland. It was a good experiement; Mrs. Staveley had done something quite remarkable. If she only had been able to take what was offered from Madame de Salzmann, Lord Pentland, and later Paul Reynard, as well as giving to her students. Keep the way open to the Source, as Lady Pentland suggested to me when I began to lead. Shortly before he died Paul Reynard told me he had given up on the Farm.

Mrs. Staveley was not the only one who consciously opposed Lord Pentland. With his promotion to lead the Work in America, Gurdjieff had put a fox in the henhouse, and still to this day the tempest he created then has been keeping the water in the teapot from becoming completely tepid.

I think the following from T. Cleary's translation of the Tao The Ching does Lord Pentland justice:

Skilled warriors of old were subtle,
Mysteriously powerful,
So deep they were unknowable.
Just because they are unknowable,
I will try to describe them:
Their wariness was as that of one
Crossing a river in winter;
Their caution was as that of one
In fear of all around.
They were as serious as guests,
Relaxed as ice at the melting point.
Simple as uncarved wood,
Open as the valleys,
They were inscrutable as murky water.

One day at Armonk, New York, they decided to eat lunch outside in the garden and wanted to bring the piano out to play music. As there was a chance of rain, they called to ask Lord Pentland what he thought. He told them to go ahead but make sure they were cleaned up by 1 pm. They had just finished lunch and moving in the piano, when the rain came pouring down. Another odd thing that was reported that day was the water in the house mysteriously went off and then turned back on during that same period of time.

Once a woman in the Work came to Lord Pentland: her husband, a group leader, was having an affair with one of the other women. Lord Pentland called the other woman in to a small room where private meetings were often held. She went in without a clue as to what the meeting was for.

When she entered the room, Lord Pentland picked up a dish with a half-eaten cookie on it. This half-eaten cookie he offered. She refused the half-eaten cookie with teeth marks imprinted in it. He insisted; she ran out in tears, having taken the meaning. And what was the meaning? It was unique for her; it was not just about an affair; it was connected with her image of herself. As she related this story to me years later, she told me that she was thankful for this lesson.

Note: Lord Pentland gave each of us Work and shocks specifically geared to our own subjectivity; so stories about these individual exchanges have a flavor that truly savored only when you can step into another person's shoes, or better yet have your own experience.

Of course, occasionally Lord Pentland got a shock from someone as well, as when a woman slapped him outside the Foundation in New York. He was known for having an interest in the ladies; many considered it a privilege to have his attentions, but some, like this young woman, apparently wanted to register her sincere regrets.

A very different reaction occurred when Carlos Castaneda first met with Lord Pentland. Castaneda, who is a very good story teller in person, didn't stop talking for a moment, perhaps preferring to use his story telling as a protective posture, so as to avoid a direct face-to-face. Lord Pentland seemed to have respect for Carlos Castaneda. And one can see that Carlos took from the Work as well as from Tai Chi to embellish his teachings and his MAGICAL PASSES. It turns out that one of my students in Tai Chi and healing, was, unknown to me at the time, apparently his Nagual Woman.

Through a Glass Darkly

I think it is clear that we are now entering a period of consequences—no longer do we have the luxury to merely stand back and hope for change, or to wait for the direction of more conscious actors.

There is help, but we will have to find and retrieve it so that we can circulate the Good, as Michel de Salzmann put it.

Lord Pentland was invited to speak to a rather isolated group in southern Oregon, led by George Cornelius, a pupil of Gurdjieff. In that talk and exchange he mentions that he hadn't heard Gurdjieff speak about a coming cataclysm or war. However, when Mr. A. asked Lord Pentland later about such an event, he was told if a cataclysm occurs, watch for me; but not in this body.

He also mentioned that the Four Corners region in the Southwest would be a good place of refuge. The Hopi Indians have continually occupied this area for over a thousand years. By chance, I live on the outermost rim of the Hopi ritual boundaries, just above the Aqua Fria River, in north central Arizona. Gurdjieff showed great interest in creating a center in the Southwest.

In ALL AND EVERYTHING Gurdjieff does what no historian has done; he juxtaposes the growth and influence of esoteric schools, of spiritual individuals with the ordinary meat of history, the cycle of wars and geologic cataclysms. Both of these are subject to Soolionensius, the tension and release of forces between celestial bodies.

One such instance of Soolionensius is the recent close approach of Mars to Earth, closer that it has been for fifty thousand years. Could this be related to the growing, apparently religiously fueled turmoil in the world; from Afghanistan and Iraq to the loss of constitutional freedoms in America?

We have collectively poked our nose into a hornets nest, and as the unrest spreads from Central Asia and the Middle East, northeastward into the Balkans and Russia, southeast to Korea and China, southwest into Pakistan and India, Indonesia, north to Europe and west to America, the future does not look rosy.

We do not see leaders capable of reconciling this deep social and religious division or controlling the greed and criminality of the multinational corporations for whom war is welcomed as a godsend.

There is little doubt that global weather, our environment is being severely tested as it becomes increasingly subject to the spiraling effects of global warming. Scientists nearly universally accept this. Hurricanes, tornadoes, drought are worsening; as half-million year old ice sheets evaporate, the effects are rapidly changing the face of our planet. What was decent habitat for man, for animals, for fauna is being lost at an alarming rate. Where will we live in the future?

For those in the Gurdjieff Work and other spiritual disciplines, the question of finding a safer environment to weather the coming storms becomes vital. Remember that Gurdjieff took his pupils with him or found them relatively safe havens during those hard days of war and revolution.

Now we come again to difficult times; there is no Gurdjieff living to lead us through them; we must do that ourselves with what guidance we are able to find. Whether we are prepared or not, the baton has been passed to us. We must create the new Ark for the Work.

Some Further Sayings of Lord Pentland

About Inner and Outer Work

– When you wish someone well, . . . you are also wishing it for yourself.

– You must realize . . . all the help you need comes from inside.

– When you have a quick mind, you are quick to anger.

On Relationships Between Men and Women

– Men are afraid of being pulled into something that they cannot escape from. Women of being dominated.

– A man who follows his own individual path will always attract women . . . even if he is a gangster.

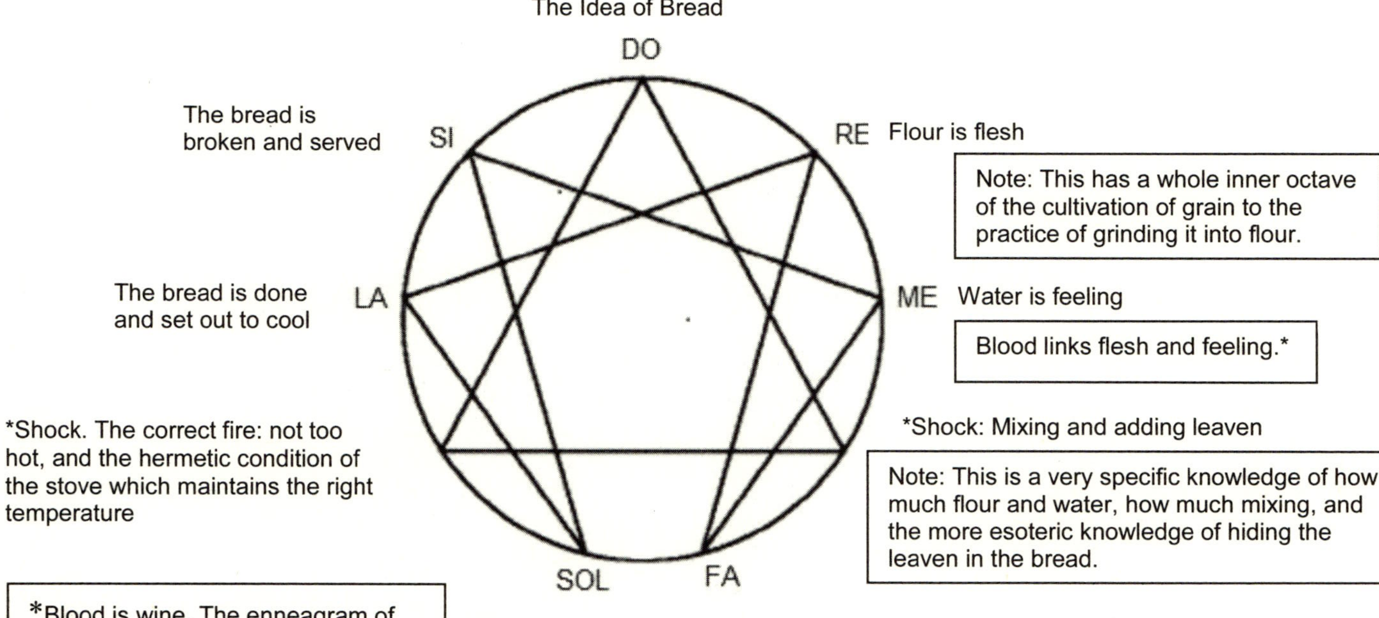

Enneagram: Baking Bread
COMMUNION—which is assimilation
The Idea of Bread
DO
The bread is
broken and served
SI
RE
Flour is flesh
Note: This has a whole inner octave of the cultivation of grain to the practice of grinding it into flour.
The bread is done
and set out to cool
LA
ME
Water is feeling
Blood links flesh and feeling.*
*Shock. The correct fire: not too hot, and the hermetic condition of the stove which maintains the right temperature
*Shock: Mixing and adding leaven
Note: This is a very specific knowledge of how much flour and water, how much mixing, and the more esoteric knowledge of hiding the leaven in the bread.
SOL
FA
*Blood is wine. The enneagram of wine will be in Volume 2.
Risen dough
The unrisen dough.
In the darkness, under damp cloth

Materialization of Thought

In the brushwork of Japan called Sumi—if a twisted blade of grass is created, there must be at least a thin strand of ink on the paper where the twist is 90 degrees to viewer. But in the Taoist tradition, the ink may be missing as long as the I (pronounced "yee") or mind intent is there. This invisible intent or thought attracts matter of another level to the stroke of the brush. It is a beginning of materialization of thought, understood by the ancient Fourth Way School of the Tao.

The attention to the brush stroke—to the hand holding the brush—through the body—carries the intention of bridging the gap—over the abyss—to materialize this bridge from an invisible Do into reality through the seven steps of the octave interpenetrated by the sacred triad of forces. This is the key to the teaching called Materializing Thought. According to Gurdjieff, it was the highest school of Egypt. In a gesture, in the vibration of the mantra Amun Ra, in the strange juxtaposition of man and animal in statues and pictures of their 'Gods' animated by ritual or Sunlight, is hidden the power of thought to influence our world.[1]

Thought at the highest level is Logos; that is, the seed from which our world continually materializes and grows. This is most lucidly shown by Jesus who is the Word made flesh. Jesus stands on the eighth and highest branch of the World Tree, with all its ramifications and levels of materiality. This World Tree shows the continual re-enactment of the original act of God.

Prometheus is forethought, thought awaiting the fresh intake of impressions. This, as opposed to his brother Epimetheus, or afterthought, represents thought as associations. Epimetheus, taking her against the advice of his brother Prometheus, was husband of Pandora, who was sent by the gods to bring confusion and despair among men. Counterpoint to this, Prometheus breaks open the forehead of Zeus opening the third eye to liberate Athena.

Thought, like Prometheus bound and chained by Zeus in the Caucasus Mountains, is thought entangled in matter, by the action of planetary forces. Thought unchained becomes both a sensitive antenna and tentacles to explore new worlds, new dimensions of reality—thought reaching out and bringing back food for thought—food for growth of Being and Reason.

Can you conceive that your hand is a thought form? For humans to function well, to be able to explore and manipulate matter on earth, this hand was needed and gradually appeared as a materialized thought fulfilling this preconceived need. All forms, a leaf, a planet, a human being are just such a manifestation of the power of seed thoughts arising from above and descending into this world 48, i.e. dying into and being reborn as a palpable reality on this lower plane. And as we are unfinished images of God we have this potential power of materializing thought—but first . . .

NOTES

[1] If the witness looks upon this frozen objective thought, in the form of an Egyptian statue, this conscious force, like sunlight can unfreeze and animate this thought form.

The Needs and Possibilities in the Development of Higher Being Bodies

Phases of Growth Needs and Possibilities	**Physical Body**	**Astral Body**	**Solar Body**	**Divine Body**
Birth—The Arising Astral Materialization	Hunger - Thirst Food H768 (DO) Water H384 (RE) Air 192 (MI) "Carriage" Medium 192 Example: Fish live in medium of water	Life Breath H192 (DO) - H96 (RE) - H48 (MI) "Horse"	Impressions H48 (DO) - H24 (RE) - H12 (MI) "Driver"	Logos - Seed Master - Witness Soul - Diamond "Master" Eternal, Unchanging Star Body
Grow Maturation Education & Vocation Conscious Labor and Intentional Suffering (FA - SO - LA)	Work Man Heavy physical labor Circulate blood Physical relations - sex, coarseness of food, sweat of your brow; strength of inner & outer muscles & organs	Healer Artist Inspiration, Myth Creative Activity The Seven Arts Cognitive Intuition Suffer for New Birth Opening Doors of Perception Psychic Sense, Feel Magnetism	Pondering on Third State of Waking Existence Symbolism, Enneagram Conscious actor, Teacher Feeding on higher hydrogens of impressions	I AM, I CAN, I DO Purgatory Cosmic Individual A Christ

continued on next page

The Needs and Possibilities in the Development of Higher Being Bodies (continued)

Phases of Growth Needs and Possibilities	Physical Body	Astral Body	Solar Body	Divine Body
Perfection—From above The crown is reason & understanding. This G. says is measured by Who (that is, what level of being) feeds on you. Complete Awareness SI*DO ⟺ DO*SI	Concentration of Forces: Si 12 Sex – Creative energy Presence through sensation of body Perfection in Presence	Develop attention Forces: Sol 12 Remember Self Connection to Higher Emotional Center Communicates with animal (bear snake) Perfection in listening	Develop meditation forces— Mi 12 To know oneself Connection to higher mind Free attention True faith is knowing Power of spiritual axis Perfection in seeing	Develop contemplation forces—H12 Wisdom A Look from Above At-one-ment I Am That I AM Crown of Reason
Qualities of Energy, Matter[1]	<u>Man</u> Man# Earth 1, 2, 3 H24 H96 H6	<u>Angel</u> Man # Planets 4 – 5 H12 H48 H3	<u>Archangel</u> Man# Solar 6 H6 H24 H1	<u>Divine</u> Man # Milky Way 7 - 8 H3 H12 H[2]
Small amounts of higher hydrogens, prana exist in the physical body and through conscious alchemy, this can be increased.	With the physical body maturing, the pre-existent pathways of energy appear that will materialize with conscious labor into astral body (using chi, prana, hanbledzoin).	So that each preceding body becomes mother/womb for the birth of the next higher body and must sacrifice its highest energy as milk to nourish child.	This milk comes from the blood of the mother. The greatest power lies in the Soul Force which is in the blood. Animated by the breath of life and guided by consciousness of the Ideal – Logos.	Harmonic Development of Man and the Path leading to the Fourth Way. Gurdjieff as the proof and living symbol of this Ark.

If I have a purpose then this precipitates new needs that arise to support functions - these needs are the materials and energies that grow and fuel and maintain these functions. Inherent in this is the realization of new qualities that are my possibilities or potential. These will change, if the challenge is met, the purpose for which I have been born into this world. And thus a triad is formed between my functions, potential and my evolving purpose each one conditioning and shaping the other.

[1] Figure 53, IN SEARCH OF THE MIRACULOUS, p. 323; [2] Hydrogen Table stepped down twice, IN SEARCH OF THE MIRACULOUS, Table 4, p. 276.

A Simplified Chart of Metamorphosis

Liberation	DO—At-onement
Rebirth	*To receive from above
Mind, Head	SI—Perfecting—Golden Light—Wheel
	LA—Completing or Return to Beginning
	*Silver Cocoon and Chamber of Metamorphosis—The soul body foetus enters deep For transformation and death
	SOL—Metamorphosis of Form—Division into Inner and Outer
	FA—Beginning of Metamorphosis
	*Awakening and Redirecting Libido/Sex Energy—SI 12 from negative and outward focused vitality to positive vitality (alchemical agent of change SOL 12 – Fire/Wish; MI 12 – Intent/Aim
Body	RE—Desire—Breathe in
	DO—Witness
↑	↑

Begin here with DO as starting the alchemical process much simplified—The struggle between desire and non-desire—The influence of wisdom teachings that show the way to reconciliation—Third Force. The creation of the transforming power of wish—The fire that heats and sublimates the creative force SI 12 (Lead into Gold) making it rise instead of descend. The wish is the heat necessary to transform! The mind places the materials to be transformed and focuses the heat. The breath strengthens the fire. The body provides the SI 12 or sex energy that has been redirected to serve the development of the soul body or astral body and this is the beginning of the process leading later to development of higher being bodies.

The Third Foundation

There is a question that arises more and more often in the hearts and minds of true seekers regarding the relation of Mr. Gurdjieff's Work leading to the Fourth Way and the current and future role of the Foundation in the fulfillment of his aims.

When one focuses on questions, often by co-incidence, by the Gods of chance, things appear that are related to one's search. In this case many such occurrences, like so many converging forces, vector and reveal something that could be of interest.

I wanted to find something diverting to read, and a book was open and out of place lying flat among some bookshelves. It was Issac Asimov's FOUNDATION'S EDGE, a book I had read years ago. I do not read much science fiction, but Asimov had always impressed me as having an exceptional mind, so I re-read it.

Now I would like to use this book as a mirror of our Gurdjieff Foundation. To make a long story short: the world had become a very complex place, and the end of the empire was near. It was an empire that contained millions of inhabited worlds, which began in a long forgotten place called Earth. Using probability theory and mentalics, a man named Seldon realized that the worlds would be in chaos for tens of thousands of years, if a plan were not created to guide people through the coming chaos.

To do this he created a Foundation whose sole purpose was to follow this plan with minimum deviation for one thousand years when a new social order would be formed. In order that this process could be adjusted from without, he created a Second Foundation unknown to the first. As with all those who come into a position of power, they would not like the idea that someone is above them, 'adjusting' their activities. This Second Foundation relied on mentalics—that is, the use of passive and active psychic properties to influence those who were in power—that is, power possessors in the First Foundation.

The principle was that the Second Foundation would use the minimum force and maximum covertness to ensure that the plan was carried out correctly.

Then there came a "fly in the ointment," something that was not predicted in the Plan, nor was it foreseen by the members of the Second Foundation. A man with very great mentalic powers called the "Mule" appeared who almost conquered the whole empire. The First Foundation with their technological advancements and the Second Foundation with their mentalics fought the Mule and finally won. This however revealed the existence of the Second Foundation. So they decided to sacrifice many of their own so that everyone would believe that the Second Foundation was destroyed. Then slowly they rebuilt in secret.

One day a man having an extraordinary ability to see into things and choose rightly—a man who was in the governing body of the First Foundation—suspected that the Second Foundation still existed and was even now pulling the strings.

Like the Wizard of Oz but with real powers, he spoke about this and was exiled because his close friend, in whom he had confided, was really an agent of the Second Foundation (not all those in powerful roles were of the First Foundation).

Many twists and turns later, upon a planet known as Gaia, a Third Foundation has long been in existence. Its powers were far beyond the first two—its wisdom and ethics—far above them. Although they have the power and knowledge, they cannot in good conscience directly interfere, but they cannot stand back as everything unravels before them.

So, gently, by encouraging certain traits and interests, they have led the main characters to a fateful encounter. A little like a fine detective story they all are gathered around the planet Gaia and the unlikely hero who has this uncanny ability to choose rightly is given the choice that the being of Gaia—which is an organic whole—planet, people, animals, plants, rocks . . . cannot itself make. Gaia gives the power even for its own destruction to this man.

Gaia places the future in his hands: to take one strand of many and follow that. Will it be the vision of the First Foundation which wishes now to bring peace and unify the worlds by strength of knowledge and technology; will it be the power of mentalics of the Second Foundation; or will it be the influence of the Third Foundation? What will he choose?

Consider the temples in Egypt or India, as Gurdjieff and others have described. They were surrounded by the more exoteric form and power structure that led invisibly inward to the mesoteric and even esoteric levels. If one were to suppose that the Foundation has many levels like that, then might not a guiding influence of a very high order still exist hidden somewhere, awaiting our deepening inquiry? If we do not open to that, what will remain, . . . merely a husk?

Ouspensky was quite correct in ordering things—novum organum, secondum organum and tertium organum, but the third came before the first.

However, it seems it is more complex than that—I have no doubt that certain past leaders succeeded in incorporating these three levels—uniting and blending them within the Temple of Man.

But returning to the present . . .

The True Nature of Thought

The tree of life (whose seed is the Logos or the father of thought) is a tree of thought.

Regarding the arousal of thought by provocation, an impression is a small bit off the tree of life. This tree is generated from the first seed or logos: branches, becoming smaller and smaller, finally reach out to us as impressions we can digest, if we are willing to make the effort to listen. This tree is speaking to us in everything we perceive: we are being fed through what we call our senses; we are being taught about the world, but we do not see it. These impressions are thought forms, and we are also thought forms—thought materialized in this time and space—at this level.

Thought descending from the Logos, from Hermes or Prometheus, is all around us and within us; we do not link these two: the power of the living thought that is outside of us with the power of the living thought that is within us. Thought becomes entangled in matter in the normal act of creation, vibration slowing down becomes material thing, and then formed into things, held captured until this relationship is reestablished. Thought becomes associations or memory: Mnemosyne (Greek: Μνημοσύνη, source of the word mnemonic) was the personification of memory in Greek mythology. A Titanide, or Titaness, she was the daughter of Uranus and Gaia, and the mother of the nine Muses by Zeus:

Calliope (Epic Poetry)
Clio (History)
Euterpe (Music)
Erato (Lyric Poetry)
Melpomene (Tragedy)
Polyhymnia (Hymns)
Terpsichore (Dance)
Thalia (Comedy)
Urania (Astronomy)

These memories are imprinted in one or more of our brains, held captive until the high God Zeus sleeps with Mnemosyne and together they birth the nine muses. Memory must be freed from its prison and serve to birth the nine (the ennea). This process involves thought disassembled and reassembling itself because of a separation between my inner and outer life.

Let us take an example from life. I am driving east from Prescott, Arizona back to my house in the Sonoran desert. Before me are enormous cumulus clouds. Underneath they are grey, blending into steel blue at the bottom. As my eyes rise to look, the grey becomes lighter and lighter until there is a luminous white at the very top.

There is this impression; it is direct (1) without interference from associations, and at the same time, I look within, for there have been other real impressions of cloud in what we call the past (2). Now intentionally I bring these two together (3), and it seems that a whole new impression arises—a kind of revelation of this cloud—and the word itself cannot contain this—it begins to expand and bursts open—(4) and so do I.

Now this word "cloud" has a totally different influence on me—in fact the experience itself was an indirect mnemonic means of not only self-remembering but of coming in contact with reality itself or, one might say, the first steps towards I AM.

So to return to the beginning: this moment of perceiving this extraordinary impression of the Nature of Cloud (1)—is connecting me to a revelation (4) of both myself and the world in which I live, that is, as Gurdjieff says "conditions." Now this contact awakens my memory sleeping in my subconscious (2) and gives birth to one or more of the nine Arts of revelation. Art meaning the linking of two or more things (3)—and this linking psychologically is spoken of in the Bible as—"when two or three are gathered in my name, there I Am."

Three forces are here simultaneously, but they must come together in me, in you; they desire to re-blend, to be whole. This is true carnal knowledge, knowledge incarnating in oneself. It is the essence of awakening, which is in fact also, a reintegration. One cannot occur without the other: psycho-energetics.

For this rebirth to occur we need foresight represented here by Prometheus, who is thought itself, descending from on high as the child of Zeus, bringing both light and heat to humankind; that is, a teaching of how to become illumined and how to transform base matter into Gold, otherwise known as alchemy. Foresight envisions this and is the catalyst for the evolution of Man against the Gods; that is, the powers and principalities that are opposed to it.

And Pandora, meaning “all gifted” with her curiosity, opens the door to a plethora of distractions so people cannot or will not focus on their true destiny. Still in the end there is hope; for "hope in consciousness is strength." (Gurdjieff)

Prometheus helps Zeus defeat time, Chronus. Then he turns his attention to Man and against the will of the Gods. For this he is tortured on a rock chained in the Caucasus Mountains. His liver (animal soul) is eaten daily by an Eagle (Zeus) and then remade to endure this same suffering for eternity.

But then a man-god Hercules, who himself has endured tremendous suffering, frees Prometheus. Think on this and free Prometheus in yourself to envision your true destiny: I repeat, it is direct (1) without interference from associations. At the next moment I consciously look within, for there have been other real impressions of cloud in what we call the past (2). Now intentionally I bring these two together (3), and it seems that a whole new impression arises—a kind of revelation of this cloud—and the word itself cannot contain this—it begins to expand and bursts open—(4) and so do I.

Memory is opposed to Lethe, the river of sleep; it was said initiates must drink of Mnemosyne which is represented as a deep pool of living memory.

Attunement (Si-Do)

All that can be accomplished by man's effort against the immense wheel of Creation—climbing through the steel gears that grind life and man into dust—dust sown onto the desolate moon. The Angel of Death must stand aside—the final Threshold!

And there is nothing I can do after these many labors, suffering, and triumph over powers and principality: I am unarmed, and only now I see that my super effort is to do nothing—to accept at-one-ment.

The Great Sun is rising and its radiance envelops me...Do-Si.[1]

NOTES

[1] "And the Stopinder which HE shortened, is between its last deflection and the beginning of a new cycle of its completing process; by this same shortening, for the purpose of facilitating the commencement of a new cycle of its completing process HE predetermined the functioning of the given Stopinder to be dependent only upon the affluence of forces, obtained from outside through that Stopinder from the results of the action of that cosmic concentration itself in which the completing process of this primordial fundamental sacred law flows.

"And this Stopinder of the sacred Heptaparaparshinokh is just that one, which is still called the 'intentionally-actualized-Mdnel-In.'"

From G. Gurdjieff, *All and Everything, First Series: Beelzebub's Tales to His Grandson* (New York: E.B. Dutton, 1950), p. 754. For the complete quote see pages 753-755.

To a question regarding Do-Si, Alan Francis replied, "Do-Si means the effort is to surrender to the force coming down from above."

Two Waking Visions

I Vision:
Summer, 1995
California

I am standing in a meadow in silence except for nature sounds of crickets and birds, wind.

Then, from the hills above, moving down along a winding trail, two beings of light appear, conversing in a melodic tongue. Although they are translucent, it is clear to me who they are: Gurdjieff and Madame. As they are walking past, they turn towards me, with a slight nod, continuing on their Way.

II Vision:
Summer, 1997
California

Again I am in this same meadow, standing now at a crossroad of trails.

One easy path leads upwards towards a crystalline house full of light and warmth. The other path, difficult and dangerous, leads downward into a canyon dark in shadows.

The inviting upper path calls; people are there; friendly voices can be heard.

But at my side, Michel appears, having descended from the hill. He points to the path below us and says we must take off our shoes and descend. So I follow him into this valley of shadows. He tells me I must walk this path every day.

Along the sheer cliff face the ground is rocky, the path narrow. Our bare feet touch the floor of the valley. We walk along for a time until we come to a cave; here he stops.

I feel that this cave is the true entrance to the Way. Michel tells me to enter.

Nine Steps to Inner Freedom

Preface

In the vast wasteland called modern life where people live in a bubble of reality, there is a symbol of the concrete and powerful forces that rule our fate. This symbol was passed down for thousands of years to real Initiates in the Great Brotherhood. Hidden from Biblical "swine," the pearls of wisdom remained inviolate. The symbol of the Enneagram was and is the representation of the pathway to the Pearl of Great Price, a Pathway to evolving wisdom.

In stark opposition are those forces that seek to inhibit human evolution. "For we wrestle not against flesh and blood, but against powers and principalities." (Ephesians 6:12) Or to paraphrase G. I. Gurdjieff, we who strive to evolve must enter the Struggle of the Magicians, and in this struggle there is no place for the Boy Scout mentality. In this place we must become "... as cunning as serpents."

To be cunning and canning, one must know something of the future–of the coming moves of those who stand in opposition, attempting to block our Way. Cunning strategies are the canning of the mind. Just as crucial, one also must have the will to overcome on the level of both physical and psychic forces.

In this spiritual warfare, there is no blind faith; this is an oxymoron; faith is, in fact, foreknowledge, as in the parable of the Centurion. So, in order that faith and will can be applied in a more precise gesture, the symbol of the enneagram, a roadmap, was created to help those who are returning to the Path.

It is not for the fainthearted or ethicist who dabbles in what "should be" and judges others; no, it is for those who have relinquished all hope in the pedantic; this talisman is for those who are willing to become riders on the storm, who strive for wisdom and power to wrestle the powers of darkness, willing to match wits and will with them on their own field of battle.

Who will go into the darkness to fight for the light? Two thousand years ago, after millennia of preparation by the Magi and others, a prince of light struggled into existence, a Christ named Jesus. But in the 2000 years since that moment when the veil was rent open, humanity has not stirred from its indolence. Humanity now rests even more comfortably in its sleep.

While all the do-gooders continue to prattle about morality and what is right, the violence and deterioration of life on Earth continues unabated. However, there are those who do not pretend, who absorb the darkness and struggle within to transform the poison into a new force for change. Swallowing this poison is not without consequence, not without risk, and it is best if the do-gooders stay far from this way of blame[1] for they have neither the stomach nor the cunning for it. To defeat the forces that are blocking Man from evolving is to put oneself in the middle of the cyclone, and to do it intentionally and so artfully that, in the end, a new Man arises.

> *There are many here among us who feel that life is but a joke. But you and I, we've been through that, and this is not our fate. So let us not talk falsely now, the hour is getting late.*[2]
>
> —Bob Dylan

The New Man

The most important tool for this effort is the Enneagram, held close in an Initiate system only to be opened to the world by the Last of the Initiates, G.I. Gurdjieff. Now those of us in Gurdjieff's direct lineage, who, through his bloodline, know the truth of this powerful and desperate struggle, take on the task he left unfinished. Everyone who Works on himself or herself seriously has the possibility of joining themselves to the Fourth Way and will find a welcoming hand here.

Look at our history and you will see the truth of it. Know the truth, and it will set you free. The Enneagram, brought from the deepest teachings of the Sarmoung Brotherhood, is a tool given to us to find, examine, and verify what is true.

Talking heads cannot and will never understand the truth of forces, the real forces, that rule our lives and of which we must take the control if we have in our essence, a real wish.[3]

The inheritors of the Sarmoung, the new Initiates, are like bees gathering the pollen from within a far radius of the hive and bringing it to a new center to be transformed into honey and royal jelly. The new substances must pass through their own body; they cannot be separate from being.

As Riders on the Storm, we learn to travel upon the river of forces rather than drown in it. We are the last of the Originals, and if a new generation does not arise now, the impulse will die. So, in this interval, I write, but only for those who can hear and who, although still mired in illusion, strive to come towards the Way.

Calling the Powers

When I begin, it is necessary to have a circle and to stand in the center, which represents the center of the World and the center of my being. Here in the center I can call the Powers to support my Work. But if I do not have a circle, an enclosure, and a center to which these forces can converge and be held, then I will never create the conditions for metamorphosis.

When my cup is full, when I feel I am right, I cannot accept the truth of my situation and cannot begin to take a step towards this center. As I awaken to my nothingness, I am in the moment of creation. Now we are speaking from the heart of the Enneagram. We cease to pretend we are someone we are not, and we cease to protect this self-image with our life.

Only a most radical approach to piercing the veil of illusion has any hope of succeeding. This approach is called The Way of the Sly Man.

Construction of the Enneagram, the Ring of Power

To understand the Enneagram we must pay attention as we construct it; as with all magical symbols, the respect we give to its construction affects the power of the symbol created and our own life. So do not take it lightly.

But let us talk more concretely. There is a circle, which represents the whole which we seek to understand through this magical process; it represents eternity—a snake biting its own tail.

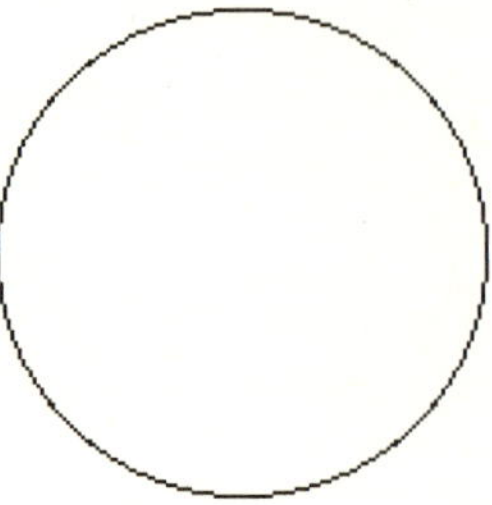

Then a triad is constructed: 3 into unity = .3333.... the unity of the cosmos which we are exploring. Start at the top, point 9: 3x3. Then go to point 3, then to 6, and back to 9. (From 9, which is affirmation, and 3, denial, we must find 6, the Holy Spirit or reconciling force.)

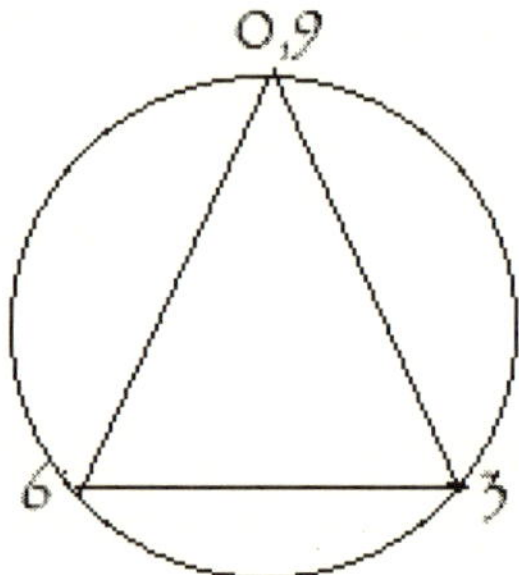

The whole is now represented and also the division into a triad of forces (as the human being is divided into three centers—Intellectual Center, Body or Moving Center, then Feeling or Emotional Center).

Next comes the 6 points of process and progression from beginning to end. Unity divided by 7 creates the sequence 1, 4, 2, 8, 5, 7 and then returns to 1. And this is the way the six pointed star is constructed. Begin at point 1, then to 4, to 2, to 8, to 5, to 7, and finally return to 1. So, we experience the Enneagram:

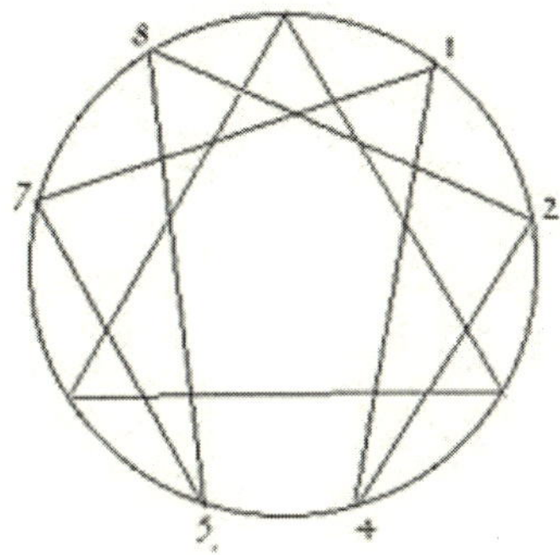

Only then the succession of 1 to 9 comes into being. It represents "the-line-of-the-flow-of-forces-constantly-deflecting-according-to-law-and-uniting-again-at-its-ends."[4]

And one more thing: when Gurdjieff had his students convert an old airplane hanger, he had a central pole installed as it was rising up from the ground. This central pole held all the constantly changing forces, where all forces converged.

Finally, when it was finished, he stood and said, "Now if we have done this right, it will hold; if not, it will all fall." He removed the center post, and it held. This was a living metaphor of our work and of the Enneagram. There is a natural subconscious need when looking at a circle to find the center of gravity; it is always there whether you mark it "consciously" or not.

When you take a step on the path, and you awaken, you are living in the moment. As Gurdjieff said, when you are in the moment, you can repair the past and prepare for the future. This idea is immensely important. It is here that we can practice a new form of reconciliation, and the meaning of the circle of repetition or eternity can be understood.

Each and every step on the path is connected by invisible radii to the center so that this temporary moment of presence becomes connected to the center, to the All and Everything, and to every other point and line of the Enneagram.

One can work with Gurdjieff's magical formula: to be in the present, one can repair the past and prepare for the future. Take a past event to repair in your own life.

This symbol is a magic talisman, a weapon against the genie of eternal sleep. It is both a sword and a shield, like the weapons of Archangel Michael, the protector of the Way.

Let us look at the Enneagram practically. The Circle must be around us (as a shield or atmosphere has been created around the Earth). This circle is a magnetic force field that protects and filters influences; i.e., separates the good from the bad. Within this circle (representing the whole of us) is a triad of forces; i.e. unity divided and reunited through the Law of Three. Here forces that transform lower energies into higher are brought together. They can be seen as inner or outer weapons to defend our unity in a kind of cosmic judo; this judo can turn forces of involution into evolution; i.e., forces of sleep and identification (that metaphorically speaking, pull us into the rocks, like Odysseus' temptation by the sirens) can be metamorphosed into strengthening our will to survive and go forward.

Finally, the six pointed star represents our wings to fly towards our aim, or the steps on the ladder to progress to the next higher level. A Do is pulled upward to the next higher level of being; i.e., from moon to earth, or earth to planetary (astral) level, and so on up the scale towards the origin of our essence designed to produce a real human being.

So, the Enneagram must be realized within us as the complete symbol of our potential and also of the areas of weakness, or identification, where we can be trapped by the enemy of the Way. When we have incorporated the Enneagram into ourselves, we are prepared in our mind, in our material body, and in our awareness to be a pilgrim on a very difficult and dangerous journey to the stars.

If we look at one well-known symbol, the cross, we see the crossing of forces, vertical and horizontal, that show us our situation. There are vertical forces that evolve or involve and horizontal forces—places of temporary stability, the level on which we live. However, in the Orthodox cross we find a third force, at the level of the feet. That is where we begin our Pilgrimage and what acts as a reconciliation between the first two forces. So the Orthodox cross is more complete, and in this diagonal line at the level of the feet, we feel the possibility of

metamorphosis. Where the two forces end in stasis, when a third force enters, a totally new direction arises.

When one begins, it is necessary to have a circle and stand in the center. Where I stand will represent the center of the world and the center of my being. Here in the center I can call the powers to support my Work. But if I do not have a circle, a cocoon, and a center to which these forces can converge and be held, then I will never create the conditions for metamorphosis.

Metamorphosis is not just ordinary change, not just transformation on a plane. Rather, it is a revolutionary step on the world axis. That step is a rising up from the Earth, from the life of a worm towards the sky, transforming into a winged being. Can you feel that underneath the flesh on your back that there are these buds of wings? Can you begin to comprehend the magnitude of change Gurdjieff was speaking about? This distance between Man #1, 2, 3 and Man #4 and 5—no we have no sensation of this, for it is another level entirely.

Standing inside the Enneagram at the center means to be physically present, yes. And a great deal of our preparatory Work is to bring our attention to the sensations which are constantly coming to us through our body. But I do not notice the life of my body, and I do not listen; therefore, nothing sticks. My life goes by, and then it ends—unless, I have begun to incorporate these energies into a new cosmic scheme that evolves from living within. Then I enter a world of myth, that is, the story of life seen from an entirely new level of Being. It is a world of the Gods as spoken about in the Bible and in the sacred books and artifacts of all cultures of the World.

But know that once you enter, there is no turning back, and the road ahead is fraught with dangers, with risk and with adventure. When you have no soul, when you exist as a machine, these powers have you in check; you are an unconscious slave. When you open your eyes and see the truth, you are also seen, both by the higher and by the planetary powers or gods who control the level to which you aspire. These gods and their offspring do not look kindly on rivals. Gurdjieff was subject to their wrath and very nearly was killed many times because he would not give up. Fortunately, he had help and an indefatigable wish to create a new ark, a new teaching to this world.

Draw a circle around you: this is like a Yezidi circle but one from which your I's cannot get out. It captures not only your I's but also subdues external influences that keep you on this level.

Now, sit in this circle at the center–holding a philosopher's stone at your center, at the abdomen–and allow the convergence of forces to bring in the I's as they are magnetized toward their home, the center. Now the three essential forces, which have been placed in you: the mind and the body, i.e., attention and the visceral sensation of our body—(sex–instinctive center and moving center) have been intentionally drawn into the circle. This is called presence; then, at the center of our being, settles calmly the essence. It is within this essence that the I will return to take command.

At the center of the Earth's sphere of influence is Man who is the bridge to the planetary world, and, at the center of Man, is essence, which is bridge to higher emotional life. At the center of essence is the I, which is the next step in the ladder to the Sun. Now, circles within circles, wheels within wheels, are turning, and as they turn, the spokes strike the notes and produce the music of the spheres. This music is the link that produces harmony in all beings and in all levels of creation; it is the spark that draws the sound upward, as fire is drawn upward.

We begin, locked into the lunar world, unable to move; but we find that the circle can work in two ways: to bind us or to free us by producing an artificial space in which a new organism can grow, a new birth, The New Man. Choose one: prison or freedom. But if you choose freedom, you must be willing to be bound to a teaching, to a Master,[5] until you have earned your freedom.

NOTES

[1] See Kathryn Hulme, *The Nun's Story* (Boston: Little, Brown and Company, 1956). pp. 1165-1166.

[2] From Bob Dylan, *All Along the Watchtower*, ©1968, 1996 by Dwarf Music,

[3] G. I. Gurdjieff, *Gurdjieff's Early Talks, 1914-1931* (London: Book Studio, 2014), pp. 351-6, esp. 353. See also Jeanne de Salzmann *The Reality of Being*. (Boston: Shambhala, 2010), Number 45,"To 'know myself,'" pp. 95-6.

[4] G. Gurdjieff, *All and Everything, First Series: Beelzebub's Tales to His Grandson* (New York: E.B. Dutton, 1950), p. 750.

[5] See P.D. Ouspensky, *In Search of the Miraculous* (San Diego, CA: Harcourt, 1977), p. 365

Alexander Salzmann's 1923 design for Institute programmes.

Exercises

for the

Development of Centers

Exercise 1
Sensory Round

Allow the body to be in a suitable sitting position. Start at the periphery and move inward; notice your sensation when you put your attention on the various parts of the body as they are mentioned.

Starting with the right arm, let attention rest on the tip section of the index finger and wait without thought until awareness of sensation develops here; then slowly move attention down finger to the place where the finger joins the palm. Leave attention there calmly and patiently until the experience of sensation in the whole finger develops. Then move attention to the middle finger and repeat the process; next, starting at the tip, sense ring finger. Then move attention to the little finger. Finally move to the thumb.

Next move the attention to the palm of the hand and then slowly to the back of the hand. Later maintaining sensation in the places already touched may be possible, but if not yet, and that is normal. See active and passive addition to this exercise (Exercise 2).

Now move the mind's gaze up arm, sensing the front and then back of wrist, lower arm, elbow, upper arm, shoulder. Is it possible yet to sense the whole arm and hand now all together?

Next, move attention to the right leg and foot. Start with the toes, with the big toe. Take time sensing all toes here and then move to the bottom of foot, the arch, and then the top of the foot. Slowly now up right leg from the right ankle, then lower leg, shin and knee, then thigh, sensing the whole circumference of this leg up to the point where it joins the hip.

Move now with attention to left leg and repeat the process with as much care and attention as from the beginning. And then go to left arm in the same manner.

In this exercise attention has moved from the periphery of body towards the central nervous system and spine. The idea is to reconnect the sensation with its source brain, the Moving Center. For this a divided attention is necessary.

Make the round counterclockwise three times.

Variation: Start (1) with right arm, then right leg, then left leg, then left arm. Move attention diagonally across from left arm to right leg in order to begin the next round (2). On this round sense right leg, left leg, left arm and, last, right arm. Then move attention from right arm diagonally across body to left leg, and do this (3) round starting left leg, then left arm, then right arm, then right leg. To complete the exercise (4), move attention diagonally first by sensing left arm, then right arm, then right leg, then left leg. You have now completed the exercise. This variation may be repeated.

Exercise 2
Addition to the Sensory Round Exercise
Aim: To develop active and passive attention.

Addition (a) of #2. Sense right arm starting with fingers and moving up to shoulder joint (moving towards the center). Then when moving to right leg; retain passive attention in right arm while moving active attention into right leg. Continue the sequence in this manner. The intensity of the attention is on the one you are moving into, concentrate active half of attention on it.

Addition (b) of #2. For an example, I can be pondering something while walking around, but I am not going to stumble over what is in my path. I am not asleep in my body while I am pondering. I will not be distracted; I will follow through and complete the octave of the exercise. Do not be an absent minded professor.

Addition (c) of #2. Do the sensory round and add a count to the sensory round with each limb. Such as counting by two's (2,4,6,8) or count by two's and three's so that you get 2-3, 4-6, 6-9,

8-12, 10-15 and keep going up to 100 and then reverse (98-97, 96-94, 94-91 . . .).

Exercise 3
An Exercise for Feeling Center
Solar Plexus

Repeat the exercise for the sensory round, but through the solar plexus and with feeling. Then simultaneously work with conscious breathing so that the breath enters the same places with the attention.

Using the conscious breath to reinforce feeling, this is then a saturation of the body with Prana to help form the Astral Body. In addition it is the linking ground between emotional center and the mind; between the horse and the driver, that is, to be sure what is called the reins.

Exercise 4
Variation on an Exercise from Lord Pentland
Note: Associations must be repulsed and emanations must be gathered and internalized to feed essence.

To retain emanations one must become like a little magnet in the center of gravity of your body, in the lower abdomen. Retain emanations in the arms 5 minutes. (Begin by sensing your arms and using your intention guided by Imagineering to control the flow of emanations. In time you may be able to see emanations—like seeing the ripples coming from a leaf that drops into a still pond.) In the legs 5 minutes. In the lower abdomen and genitals, in the chest, in the head, in the whole of one's body. In the beginning retain emanations ¼ inch from the body, and then later as the strength of one's presence increases, let this expand outwards for several inches, but always a definite distance up to a hand's length.

The physical body moves the blood in a heartbeat, but there are also inner vibrations from the heart that are rippling outward as emanations. The heart is just an example so that we might be able to begin to perceive more easily, but everything is emanating: the cells, organs, everything.

Exercise 5
Concentration, Attention, Meditation, Contemplation

(1) Left hand index finger: Push the left index finger from shoulder (a); pointing straight out at shoulder height from the body to arm's length (b); (say "concentration").

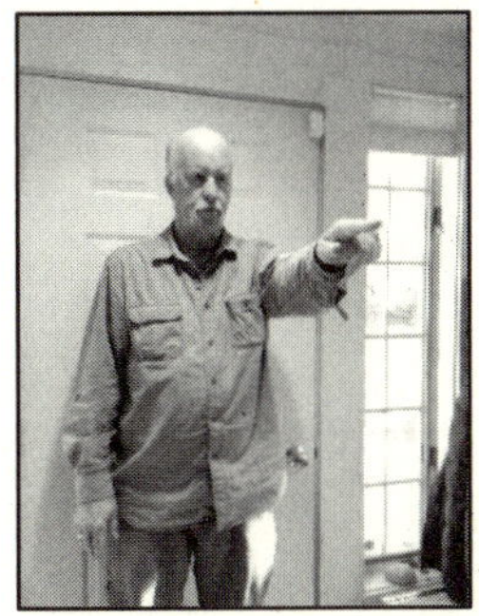

(2) Right hand index finger pointing out straight at arm's length (c) moves to the left to join left pointing index finger (at b).

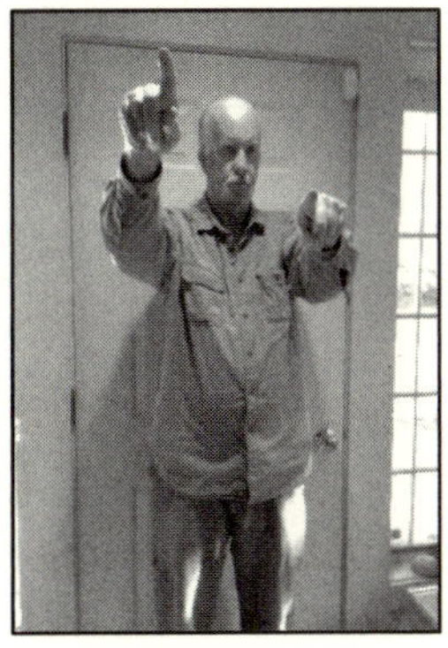

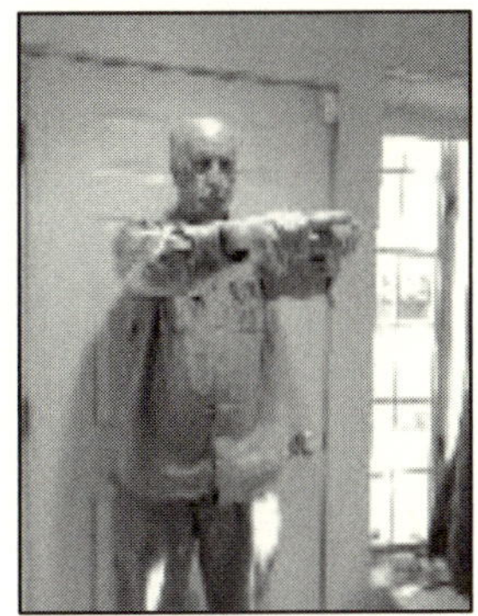

(3) Return left hand towards origin (a) and right hand to origin (c) (say "attention").

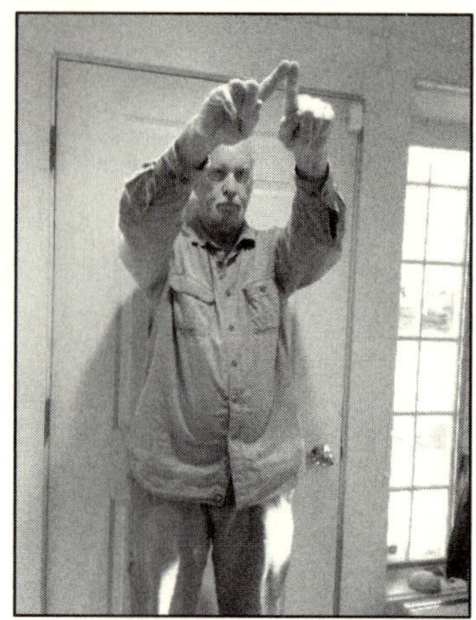

Continue this movement: "concentration, ... attention; concentration ... attention." Do this 7 times.

(4) With fingers spread apart bring them up to close the triangle at the apex (d). (Say "meditation"). (5) Now combine these steps together 7 times. On the 8th time visualize the center of the triangle (e). Drop the hands to the sides and say the word "contemplation."

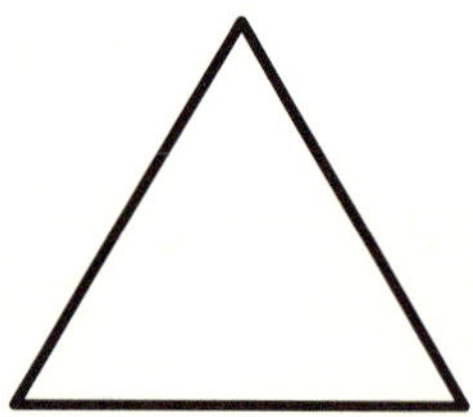

Addition: Replace the words with "I," "Am," "Can," "Wish."

Exercise 6
Triangle and Square

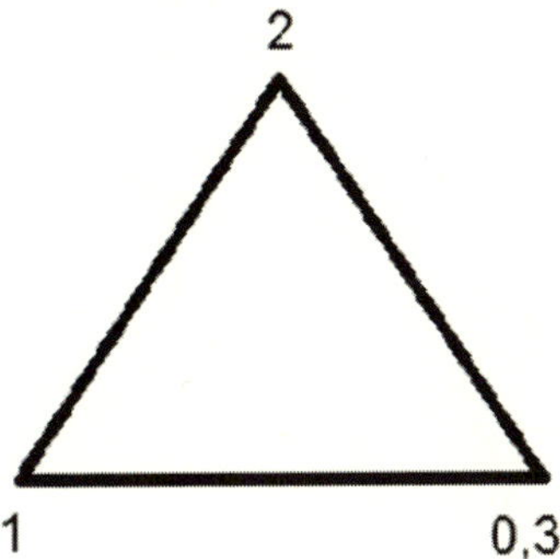

With left hand, index finger as pointer, inscribe in the air an equilateral triangle, starting at the bottom right hand side. Start at 0,3 and move to the left to point 1. Then up to the top (middle over bottom line) to point 2 and back to join up the lines to triangle to point 3. As you move you count,"1, 2, 3."

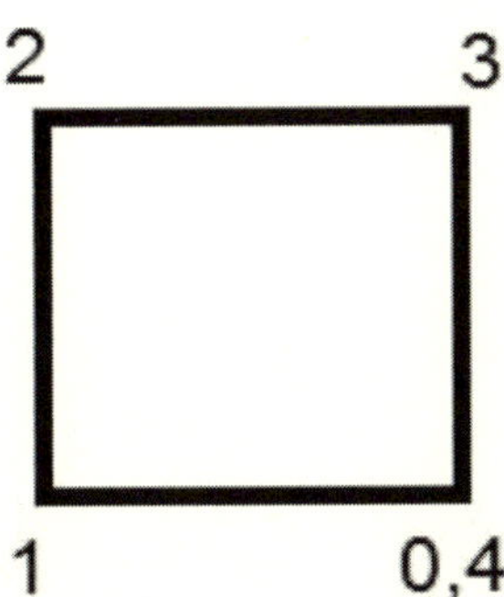

With the right hand, beginning in the right lower corner (0), start with point 0, moving to the left (in the same direction that you did the triangle, i.e., moving clockwise) and counting to point 1. Then straight up to point 2; then straight across moving to the right to point 3, and down to point 4 to close the square (at 0,4).

Do the two simultaneously, triangle, square, on the count 1, 2, 3, 4 – so that on the triangle you complete one circuit and continue one step further. Continue this on multiples of 7, up to 49 times.

Next addition: Close left eye and do triangle looking from the right eye. Now close the right eye; do square with the right hand looking from left eye.

Advanced: Slight cross open eyes and do preceding exercise simultaneously, so left eye is following the right hand; the right eye is following the left hand.

Note: If you try this advanced addition, do it for only a short time because it may cause headaches until you learn how to relax.

When you finish, close your two eyes and let your attention resonate with the pineal gland, also known as the Third Eye.

Exercise 7
Infinity Symbol
∞

For left-right brain balance

Note: do each part for a few minutes.

With index finger of your left hand inscribe in the air the infinity symbol. Then do it with your right hand. Then do it simultaneously in the same direction following carefully with both eyes. Then reverse direction–again with both hands moving in the same direction. Then, do them in opposing directions.

With eyes open, breathe in "I" as you come inward; breathe out "Am" as you go outward.

Exercise 8
Axis of Attention Numbers 1 and 2
(Rocking Exercise Rocking 1 and 2 Cocoon)

Sitting upright in a chair, not leaning against the back support, feet close enough so that one can easily move to a standing position (test this so you are sure you can stand stably):

Top of head is aligned with the base of the spine, as though pulled up from the top of the head so that the vertebrae hang loosely from the top, palms of the hands on the knees, mind clear of thought.

Preparatory exercise: Rock back and forth on you ischial (sitz) bones, the oscillation of the head about two inches as you rock. Rock back and forth seven times while intentionally projecting your image so that on the seventh time you will slip into that image and be standing. Pause there for seven breaths and sit down again in the same way.

Beginning exercise: You will rock back and forth 49 times. From the center below the abdomen project through the top of the head the image of your body moving from a sitting to a standing position. You will maintain this projection rigorously; on the 49th rock forward you will allow your body to enter into this projection, and rise up through it until you are actually in a standing position. Count seven breaths. As you do this, you will be projecting yourself back into the sitting position, and on the seventh, you enter into that projection and sit precisely.

Addition: As you rock backwards, say "I"; forward, say "Am"; breathing in "I" and out "Am." As you project your body, project "I Am" within the body. Continue with "I Am" through the seven breaths standing, and then come back down into the sitting position.

Part (2) of #8: Repeat exercise picturing yourself rising through the top of your head. This strengthens embryonic energy body—then the physical body rises to engage it—like a hand entering a glove (image from Lord Pentland). The projection acts like a magnet to draw the physical into the Astral. This strengthens the Astral and it is a means to counter the effect of Heropass by intending through time.

Exercise 9
Subconscious

Lie comfortably without anything causing distraction on bed or floor with mat. Focus your attention like a thread of light. Then with your intention let your heartbeat and breath slow down; consciously aware, attach the thread of attention to the descending beat of the heart and breath. The body begins to move towards a state of sleep, but even as you move into sleep, the light at the end of the thread of attention remains bright. I remain awake as I enter my subconscious, my essence, and in this state I can begin to search out who am I. Do not slip into dream.

Move advanced techniques regarding these and other exercises will appear in Volume II.

Exercise 10
Reintegrating the Emotional Center

Start standing in upright position, head straight. Raise left arm, palm up about six inches above head while lowering right arm, palm down to lower abdomen level. Then turn palms in opposite direction facing each other as if holding a circle.

Put left palm to heart, attempting to sense/feel its beat. Once picked up, begin to move this hand very lightly forward and back in a light patting gesture as if reinforcing the beating heart.

Bring right palm to solar plexus level, over the solar plexus, about one inch away from solar plexus. When right hand has picked up emanations of solar plexus, it begins to move and spi-

•

rals outward to four inches from body and then back again, close to the solar plexus.

Both hands are moving with a feeling that a magnet is inside of them at the center of the palms, drawing out a portion of the essence of the heart and the solar plexus. Each step in the process should take several minutes guided not so much by a measure of time, but by a measure of the feeling in constatation of completion of each phase of the process.

Reverse hands so that the left hand is gently patting the area of the solar plexus and the right hand is spiraling near the heart, directing the stored energies in the hands back into the heart and solar plexus, thus reintegrating the two halves of the emotional center.

Turn the right palm up and the left palm down, the right hand rising above the head and the left palm moving to the lower abdomen simultaneously to complete the circuit as above so below.

Addition: When patting the heart and spiraling from the solar plexus, breathe in "I Am." Breathe out "Wish." when you reverse hands, breathe out "I Am"; breathe in "Wish."

Exercise 11
Reinforcing the Psychological with the Energetic to Dissolve Kundabuffer

(First Exercise in New Cycle)

Counteracting and deconstructing the effect of Kundabuffer—the mechanics of illusion—Gurdjieff tell us to "Bear the negative manifestations of others" as the best and safest means to gradually dissolve Kundabuffer's effects. He indicates that Buddha also recommended this, but this vital teaching was quickly lost among Buddha's followers, and the opposing conditions were instead embraced—that of immurement like a hermit. One understands that this could also mean walling oneself off from people so that it is possible to be with people and still isolate oneself, only pretending to bear their unpleasantness.

To accelerate the process that Gurdjieff recommended, making it more possible to have a concrete result, it is necessary to combine and synergize the energetical with the psychological. Now the effect of the psychological is twofold; the first is to compel the false mechanical and egoistic reaction and the I's they inhabit to reveal themselves, and the second is to turn up the heat so the false or chaff is burned away.

This is a long and uncomfortable process. Few take it to the end, and therefore complete destruction is not accomplished. As it might be said, after you sweep one devil from the house, the resulting vacuum, if not filled consciously, is instead filled with seven demons each worse than the first.

Thus, the Sly Man can improve and accelerate this conservative approach by supplementing the heat derived from psychological friction with heat generated through focused breathing into the blood and Astral energies or Prana. This is not hyperbole; there is an actual change in the temperature of the body. This can be understood through reading the "Energy Pathways Handbook." Do this in conjunction with recollecting the negative manifestation of another person or even more potent, while you are intentionally turning the cheek, in life.

In this method the energetic fire potentiates the psychological friction focused on the base of the spine with the precise aim of melting down the core of Kundabuffer's influence. Creating fire otherwise without this aim and guiding wisdom produces nothing but useless and destructive suffering because the ego is not restrained.

In volume 2 we will work with the 101 methods of retarding the influence of Kundabuffer.

Exercise 12
Prepare the Soil; Sow the Seeds

Preparatory Instructions
(from LIFE IS REAL ONLY THEN, WHEN 'I AM'[1])

First, all one's attention must be divided approximately into three equal parts; each of these parts must be concentrated on one of the three fingers of the right or the left hand, for instance the forefinger, the third and the fourth, constating in one finger—the result proceeding in it of the organic process called "sensing," in another—the result of the process called "feeling," and with the third—making any rhythmical movement and at the same time automatically conducting with the flowing of mental association a sequential or varied manner of counting.

For this fourth preparatory exercise explained by me today, first of all it is necessary to learn with what exists in you now only as a substitute, so to say "fulfilling the obligation" of what should, in real man, be "self-willed attention" and in you is merely a "self-tenseness," simultaneously to observe three heterogeneous results proceeding in you, each coming from different sources of the general functioning of your whole presence: namely, one part of this attention of yours should be occupied with the constatation of the proceeding-in-one-finger process of "sensing," another with the constatation of the proceeding-in-another-finger process of "feeling," and the third part should follow the counting of the automatic movement of the third finger.

Preparation (A)

On right hand index finger only—sensation. Stop (this finger).

Go to middle finger—feeling. Stop (this finger).

Third finger—head, rhythm and count. Stop (this finger).

Then, do first and second fingers. Stop (these two fingers).

Then do second and third fingers. Stop (these two fingers).
Then do first and third fingers. Stop (these two fingers).

Then, when you have accumulated sufficient attention, do all three fingers as indicated above.

Part B

Do same on left hand.

Part C

The intention is to be able to be attentive to each of the three fingers on the right hand and to the centers from which the impulses in them arise: The first finger connecting with my own spine and the reptilian brain; the second with the solar plexus, and the third with the head. If you are sensing the index finger, that sensation arises in the moving center (the spine and reptilian brain), so it is possible to follow it back to the center from which it arose. The same is also possible for the emotional and intellectual center that you can follow the trail back to the source like a hunting dog following a scent trail.

Now do left hand.

Then, do left and right hand together with centers.

The three levels of impressions are passive; the attention from each center, active. Find the reconciling force as you hold these two simultaneously, completing the circuit consciously—between inner and outer worlds.

NOTES

[1] G. I. Gurdjieff, *All and Everything, Third Series: Life is Real Only Then, When 'I Am'* (London: Arkana Triangle Editions, 1978), pp. 113, 114-115.

Afterword

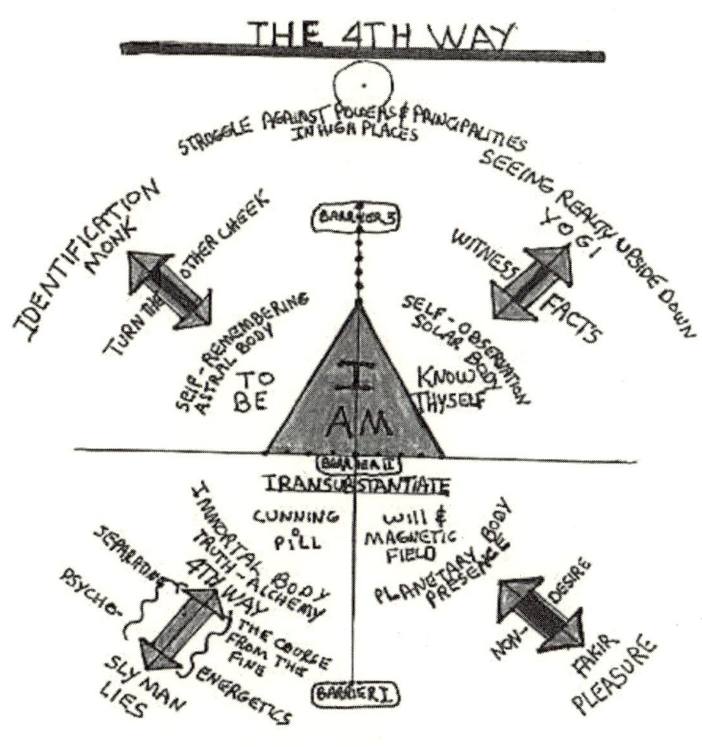
THE 4TH WAY
STRUGGLE AGAINST POWERS & PRINCIPALITIES IN HIGH PLACES
SEEING REALITY UPSIDE DOWN
YOGI
WITNESS
FACTS
IDENTIFICATION
MONK
TURN THE OTHER CHEEK
BARRIER 3
SELF-REMEMBERING ASTRAL BODY
TO BE
I AM
SELF-OBSERVATION SOLAR BODY
KNOW THYSELF
BARRIER II
TRANSUBSTANTIATE
IMMORTAL BODY
TRUTH-ALCHEMY
4TH WAY
CUNNING PILL
WILL & MAGNETIC FIELD
PLANETARY BODY
PRESENCE
SEPARATION
PSYCHO-
THE COURSE FROM THE FINE
SLY MAN
LIES
ENERGETICS
BARRIER I
NON-DESIRE
FAKIR
PLEASURE
OUTER DARKNESS